MW00943572

Shining Out
and Shining In

Dear Colleen
Thanks for you
Love
ENJOY

Tom

Handwritten inscription, illegible.

Shining Out
and Shining In

Understanding the Life Journey of Tom Tipton

James R. Newby

authorHOUSE®

AuthorHouse™ LLC
1663 Liberty Drive
Bloomington, IN 47403
www.authorhouse.com
Phone: 1-800-839-8640

© 2013 by James R. Newby. All rights reserved.

No part of this book may be reproduced, stored in a retrieval system, or transmitted by any means without the written permission of the author.

Cover photos courtesy of Todd Buchanen at toddbuchanen.com

Published by AuthorHouse   10/09/2013

ISBN: 978-1-4918-1918-0 (sc)
ISBN: 978-1-4918-1919-7 (e)

Library of Congress Control Number: 2013917007

Any people depicted in stock imagery provided by Thinkstock are models, and such images are being used for illustrative purposes only.
Certain stock imagery © Thinkstock.

This book is printed on acid-free paper.

Because of the dynamic nature of the Internet, any web addresses or links contained in this book may have changed since publication and may no longer be valid. The views expressed in this work are solely those of the author and do not necessarily reflect the views of the publisher, and the publisher hereby disclaims any responsibility for them.

Contents

Why should I feel discouraged, why should the shadows come,
Why should my heart be lonely, and long for heav'n and home,
When Jesus is my portion? My constant friend is He:
His eye is on the sparrow, and I know He watches me;
His eye is on the sparrow, and I know He watches me.

I sing because I'm happy, I sing because I'm free,
For His eye is on the sparrow, and I know He watches me.

"His Eye Is On the Sparrow"

Civilla D. Martin, Lyricist

Charles H. Gabriel, Composer

Dedicated to Tom's family, and his faith communities—
Lord of Life Lutheran Church in Minnesota
and the Crystal Cathedral in California.

ACKNOWLEDGMENTS

There are many people in my life who have affected me in incredible ways. Because you have influenced my life, you have influenced this book. Stories of your impact flood the pages that follow. It is here, on this page, that I want to acknowledge not only those people mentioned in this book but literally the thousands of others not listed by name. You have shaped my love of my fellow man; you have shaken my hand and welcomed me into your lives; we have shared miracles together; we have traveled together; we have sung together, and we have prayed together. You know who you are. You are not forgotten. You are treasured for walking beside a very thankful man through 80 years of discovery, wonder, growth, and love.

In the beginning of these acknowledgments, I must first start with my dear friend, Dr. James R. Newby, who put all of this together using his gifts from God. Jim and I have had many conversations together. Besides the fact that he knows the Bible backward and forward, he is a good friend. Jim has put my whole life in perspective, as only he could. Thank you, Jim!

Jim Newby and I are grateful to the faith community of The Church of the Savior in Oklahoma City for their encouragement of this project, the office manager for her editing expertise, and especially to Greg and Francy Palmer, members of The Church of the Savior. The Palmers were gracious and hospitable during the development of this book, offering their Colorado mountain cabin for writing.

This biography would not have been possible without the financial encouragement of the following patrons. Jim and I are most grateful to Mrs. Estelle King. Estelle has been an important encourager, and it was through her husband, Harold King, that I was invited for the first time to sing at the Wayzata Community Church in Wayzata, Minnesota. Paul and Mary Webster have also been generous with their support. Paul was responsible for encouraging me to speak at the Wayzata community-wide

Prayer Breakfast in the fall of 2011. Finally, we are grateful to Mrs. Suzanne Jackson. Sue has been a generous supporter of many important projects in the Twin Cities area, as well as of her alma mater, Earlham College in Indiana. Jim Newby was on the faculty of the Earlham School of Religion, and it was this Earlham connection that was the genesis of the friendship that Sue and the author have shared for many years. *Thank you* to all of our patrons!

To the members of my board and my personal support team: I thank you for your constant flow of ideas, your stimulating conversations, your public relations work on my behalf, your financial support, and foremost for sharing your personal faith journeys with me. Thank you David Durenberger, Debbie Estes, David Frauenshuh, Paul Jones, Dennis McGrath, Jim Ramstad, Lois Rand, the late James Reynolds, Dennis Schulstad, and Wheelock Whitney, Jr.

Pastor Peter Geisendorfer-Lindgren is my pastor, friend and soul brother. His family, wife Karen, son Matt and daughter Elizabeth have been important spiritual forces in my life. They have also taken me in as a member of their family, sharing holidays and celebrations throughout the year.

Lori Schwartz is my close friend and personal manager. She has a heart of gold. She is a dedicated staff member at Lord of Life and she is as close to me as my heart. She can do anything brilliantly. She keeps me going—supporting and encouraging my work, watching my health, and feeding my spirit through art and music. We enjoy driving each other crazy. She has two incredible daughters, Kara and Kelsey, and a loving husband, Steve. I am sure Lori is largely responsible for the continuation of my life journey following my health problems in 2010. Thank you for your hours of questions, text and photography edits, research, archiving of my "life scrapbook," and organizing the publication of this book.

Thank you also to all of my "helpers" that make my everyday life easier: Simone and Janna for typing my words and writing letters, Dara for her help in the final review of the book, Jordan for my audio work, Jane for being a friend and driver, Jodie for making me presentable, Dr. Nord and Dr. Salmella for keeping me upright and smiling, Xanthe for making all of my travel easier, Eugenia for a lot of elbow grease, and the office staff of Lord of Life and the Birchwood. To all of you, thank you for being part of my life.

And of course thank you to my beautiful daughters, Cassandra, Beverly and Saintanne for your love and support.

May you take from this story the knowledge that through God all things are possible!

Blessings!
Your favorite hymn singer,
Tom Tipton

AUTHOR'S PREFACE

He looked like one of the kids on the basketball court—a seventy-seven-year-old, six-foot, four-inch kid! He was taking shots and passing the ball around to anyone who was near. He loved the game. He had played against Elgin Baylor as a child and other famous artisans of the sport when he was younger, and he went to college on a basketball scholarship. His body, however, showed the wear and tear of an aging athlete, and he required frequent sessions in a whirlpool bath just to keep mobile. But he still loved the game.

Tom Tipton was not in Oklahoma City to shoot baskets with the kids (although I think he may have preferred this!). Instead, he was at the Church of the Savior, where I am currently the Senior Minister, to share his vocal talent with us and to help kick off a million-dollar capital campaign to eliminate a building debt. He was there for the weekend at my invitation. The week before, Tom had sung the National Anthem before 60,000 Minnesota Vikings fans in the Hubert H. Humphrey Dome in Minneapolis, and on this Saturday morning, he was singing the National Anthem to a hundred elementary school children in Oklahoma City. On both occasions, Tom put forth his best.

I had first become acquainted with Tom Tipton when he came to Wayzata Community Church in Wayzata, Minnesota, to share his musical talent with the congregation. I was the minister for faith and learning at the time, and I observed his ministry of music from one of the chairs at the front of the congregation. "What a friend we have in Jesus," he would sing and slowly walk up and down the aisles, shaking hands and bringing smiles to everyone he would greet. "All our sins and griefs to bear." His rich voice filled the room, and all were touched by the passion that flowed from his heart through his vocal chords. Tom Tipton can sing anything, but he excels in the old hymns. "My life revolves around the old hymns." he told me. Watching him sing these hymns is, indeed, an uplifting and truly amazing experience.

Tom Tipton does not want this book written for his own self-aggrandizement. He wants it written because he is an encourager and wants his life story to be an encouragement to others. Although he has been released from the pain that he experienced throughout much of his life, he will belong to the fellowship of those who bear the mark of pain for as long as he lives. He is an *overcomer*, and he wants to encourage others to rise above their own difficult life circumstances to be the best that they can be.

It was Dr. Albert Schweitzer who wrote, "He who has been delivered from pain must not think he is free again, and at liberty to take life up just as it was before, entirely forgetful of the past. He is now a man 'whose eyes are open' with regard to pain and anguish, and he must help to overcome those two enemies (so far as human power can control them) and to bring to others deliverance which he himself enjoyed."

Although Tom has moved far beyond the humble life of an African-American child growing up in segregated Washington, DC, he does not, nor can he ever, escape it entirely. Each time that Tom looks into a mirror, he is reminded of his past—a past that travels through some of the most difficult times in American history.

The title of this book comes out of Tom Tipton's life experience "shining out" as a shoe-shine boy in front of the White House, the U.S. Capitol, and the Washington Monument while he was growing up and "shining in" years later inside the White House, giving a vocal performance before President Jimmy Carter and again later for President Bill Clinton.

I am grateful for the opportunity to write this biography with Tom. It is a privilege to share through the ministry of writing this remarkable life with others—a life that begins as a child in segregated Washington, DC, and is still being lived out in 2013 in the Twin Cities of Minnesota. It would be a mistake to suppose that Tom Tipton's biography is just one more in the array of books that represent the cult of personal exposure. His is different in kind. His message is one of encouragement to the thousands of persons who are now discouraged. His story belongs in one sense to the literature of witness, but in a far deeper sense, it belongs to the literature of hope. It is my hope that those who read these words will have their own lives enriched, in the same way that Tom Tipton has enriched so many lives through his ministry of music. He is an amazing man who has the gift of bringing out the best in others. Prepare for a spiritual experience.

James R. Newby
Newbeginnings
Oriental, North Carolina

Prologue—"Shining Out"

This is my Father's world:
Oh let me ne'er forget
That though the wrong seems oft so strong,
God is the Ruler yet.

"This Is My Father's World"
Text: Maltbie Davenport Babcock, 1858–1901
Music: Franklin L. Sheppard, 1852–1930

In April of 2009, the first black President, Barack Obama, and First Lady Michelle Obama hosted the annual Easter Egg Roll on the White House lawn. It was an event open to all children of different races. This was not always so. It wasn't until 1953, during the tenure of President Dwight D. Eisenhower, that the First Lady, Mamie Eisenhower, opened the Easter Egg Roll to all children, including children of color. Until this time it was a segregated event, reserved primarily for children from wealthy families. As a small boy, Tom Tipton knew none of this when he first tried to attend the annual celebration.

Before he was nine years old, Tom Tipton already had three jobs. After school and on weekends Tom would shine shoes for ten cents a shoeshine. Washington, DC, was a city of well-shined shoes, especially around the entire National Mall. On Saturdays, along with shining shoes, he worked in a flower shop and sold magazines. One spring day as he worked outside the White House, Tom heard some people talking about a children's activity that was to take place on the following Monday. Tom assumed that all children would be welcome at what turned out to be the annual Easter Egg Roll on the White House lawn. As Tom told the story, "I went to the White House in my best Sunday clothes, looking forward to a fun day. When I went up to the gate where the children and their families were being admitted, a White House guard would not let me in. He told me that I did not belong there and that I should leave. At the time, I was ignorant of prejudice, and so I was dumbfounded by not being allowed in." Tom ran home to his mother and told her what had happened. She said to Tom, "Junior, don't worry. Just love everybody." This response to his White House rejection did not satisfy Tom, and so he went to talk to his father. His father's response to young Tom was similar to his mother's. "Junior, don't worry about that. Just be the best shoeshine boy that you can be."

On the Tuesday morning following the Easter Egg Roll, Tom went back to his regular shoe shining spot in front of the White House, and from outside the iron fence, he pointed at it and said out loud, "One of these days I will be back, and I will go inside that big White House, and they will call me Mr. Tipton."

Where does an 8-year-old reach to come up with a personal challenge like that? It comes from the bottom of his soul, no doubt. How can a child even dream of working toward a goal so far-fetched? His parents could only wipe his tears and dream of a better tomorrow. How can a man pursue such a lofty goal his entire life? He is driven with a gnawing persistence, a childlike simplicity of faith, and more than a little help from his friends.

CHAPTER ONE

GROWING UP IN SEGREGATED WASHINGTON, DC

Have we trials and temptations?
Is there trouble anywhere?
We should never be discouraged.
Take it to the Lord in prayer!

"What A Friend We Have In Jesus"
Text: Joseph Scriven, 1820–1886
Music: Charles C. Converse, 1832–1918

Thomas Henry Tipton, Jr. was born June 15, 1933. Franklin Delano Roosevelt had just been inaugurated president for his first term in March, and the Great Depression was affecting every area of American life. Twenty-five percent of the American people who wanted work could not find it, and the continuing drought in the Midwest heightened the effects of the Dust Bowl. Across the Atlantic, this was the year that Adolf Hitler became Chancellor of Germany, and the first concentration camp at Dachau was opened. At 217 S Street NW in Washington, DC, they celebrated the birth of a new baby boy, a child who would grow up to be known as "America's Hymn Singer."

During the time that Tom Tipton was growing up, Washington, DC, was a segregated city. African Americans could not eat at downtown lunch counters. If they were allowed to do so, they had to remain standing. They were not allowed to see a play at the "whites only" National Theatre just a few steps from the White House. A city that became a haven for freed slaves following the Civil War was also a haven for powerful southern politicians

1

who were proud of their efforts to keep the races separate. Ruled by Congress, our nation's capital was no more integrated in the 1940s than Jackson, Mississippi, or Montgomery, Alabama. When Tom Tipton was a boy in Washington, the head of the District of Columbia panel that ruled the city was a senator from Mississippi named Theodore Bilbo, perhaps best known as a member of the Ku Klux Klan and the author of *Take Your Choice, Segregation or Mongrelization.*

Family Background

Tom's mother left his father when Tom was only two years old. Throughout his mother's eighty-seven years on this earth, she would marry five different times. When Tom arrived, she moved with her child to 231 O Street, her mother's home, just across the street from Dunbar High School. As Tom remembers the home on O Street, "It was a very warm, small, and tender home with a little front yard and a little back yard. It had an upright piano and a buffet in the dining room where Grandpa kept the Old Granddad and the Jim Beam. No one touched it but him!

"My mother was the greatest human being I have ever known in my life," said Tom, "but she was a diva. She had a closet the size of a full room filled with beautiful gowns. She would change her apparel after every other song that she would sing." Her audiences loved her many costume changes, which consisted of long, flowing gowns. She made history this way. Born in 1911, Lucille Lewis took pride in being Americas's first African-American gospel radio announcer in the nation. She was on WOOK, WUST, WOL, and WYCB radio stations from 1952 until 1998. Although she won the citywide typing championship and went to nursing school, all that she ever wanted to do was to sing, play and listen to music.

In the Congressional Record of July 31, 1998, just following her death, Tom's mother is remembered by the Honorable Eleanor Holmes Norton, the Representative of the District of Columbia. In part, she said, "Mr. Speaker, I rise today to celebrate the life and mark the passing of Dr. Lucille Lewis Tipton Banks Robinson Miller. Dr. Miller was born in the District of Columbia. She was the eldest of six daughters born to Deacon Edward Lewis and Deaconess Mary Lewis of the Metropolitan Baptist Church. As an adult, Dr. Miller became affiliated with Corinthian Baptist Church. Most recently, she was a member of the New Bethel Baptist Church. She was the devoted mother of three sons: Thomas Tipton, Arthur Robinson, and Reginald Robinson.

Caption: Lucille Lewis Tipton Banks Robinson Miller — Age 78

"Dr. Miller graduated from Armstrong High School . . . She attended Howard University, where she majored in music and minored in psychology. Dr. Miller received an Honorary Doctorate from Virginia Seminary and college in 1983, and an Honorary Doctorate from Washington Saturday College in 1996.

"With a deep love for gospel music, she formed the Banks Seminary Choir in 1937. That group rapidly became one of the most successful youth choirs in the Washington area. Following this success, Dr. Miller founded the Paramount School of Music, one of the largest private schools in the area. As she gained popularity among churches and ministries in the Washington area, Dr. Miller was called upon to be the Mistress of Ceremonies at area churches and for major gospel events. Known for her colorful and inspirational style, Dr. Miller became a legend in her own time. It was this same personal style that led her to become Washington's premier gospel music personality.

BANKS' SEMINARY CHORUS OF SEMINARY, VIRGINIA

1939

Banks' Seminary Chorus
(Lucille is standing in middle, Tom over her left shoulder in white shirt.)

"During her career, Dr. Miller received over six hundred awards and commendations and was received in an audience with Pope John Paul II in Vatican City. Two of her most cherished awards were her induction into the Thomas Dorsey Gospel Music Hall of Fame in 1996, and the Eta Beta Sorority Hall of Fame in 1996."

Lucille with Pope John Paul II

All of the major gospel singers of her time would eventually make it on Lucille's radio shows, including these legends:

- Sallie Martin belonged to Thomas Dorsey's choir, Dorsey being the "Father of Black Gospel Music" and a great

5

hymn writer. Sallie is remembered as one who performed as an inspirational preacher. She did not impress with vocal skills, but she did catch hold of the spirit in the room.

- Mahalia Jackson, the most incredible gospel singer, absorbed all of the music that her hometown of New Orleans could offer. She was drenched in the blues, and inspired by Willie Mae Ford Smith. "She gave me love and gave me a lot of Jesus," said Tom. "She showed me the overwhelming power and strength that the love of music and love of the Lord created."
- Roberta Martin, although she was not related to Sallie Martin, was a Thomas Dorsey disciple of the early 1930s. Roberta teamed up with Sallie for a brief time, using some of the best young male singers to form the Martin and Martin Gospel Singers.
- James Cleveland was the driving force behind the creation of the modern gospel sound, and was known as the "King of Gospel Music."
- Willie Mae Ford Smith was originally from Rolling Fork, Mississippi, and was reared in Memphis. She joined the family quartet, called the Ford Sisters, in 1922. "They were more like the spiritual version of the Mills Brothers," said Willie Mae. She was one who never sold out, and loved singing for the satisfaction of working for her Lord and Savior. She has been referred to as a "Gospel Saint."

Other famous gospel groups who surrounded Tom's mother included The Dixie Hummingbirds, The Golden Gate Quartet, The Harmonizing Four and The Mighty Clouds of Joy. They all loved Dr. Miller. Tom could remember each of these and many more amazing talents coming to his home and his mother's studio. He especially had fond memories of Willie Mae Ford Smith, who would hold him in her arms and rock him in church when he was a little boy.

During a recent visit to Oklahoma City, Tom sang at the Church of the Savior and referred to a gospel song that was made famous by Willie Mae—"Just a Little More Faith and Grace." When I found it on YouTube, Tom was moved to tears and began singing with her.

In an article for the *Washington Post,* Hamil R. Harris wrote about the funeral for Tom's mother that took place at Greater Mt. Calvary Holy Church in 1998. The article was titled "Singers Raise Voices in Praise of Gospel Mother." He writes, "Worshipping God while dressed in thousand-dollar sequins-over-lace gowns, glass pumps, and hair coiffured like Carol Channing isn't usual behavior for elderly church women. Her funeral was graced by the presence of twenty-two African-American ministers and one white minister . . . Rev. Robert A. Schuller from the Crystal Cathedral in California and his wife, Donna.

"But nothing was usual about Lucille Tipton Banks Robinson Miller, the sassy 87-year-old gospel radio diva who for more than four decades pumped area churches with love and glamour that kept people blushing . . .

"Miller died of leukemia on Monday, and last night more than a thousand people, including a number of legendary artists, came out to a foot-stomping Gospel Celebration."

"Then shall the King say unto them on His right hand, come, ye blessed of my Father, inherit the kingdom prepared for you from the foundation of the world: For I was hungered, and ye gave me meat. I was thirsty, and ye gave me drink: I was a stranger, and ye took me in: Naked, and ye clothed me: Verily I say unto you, In as much as ye have done it unto one of the least of these my brethren, ye have done it unto me."   Matthew 25: 34-36, 40

Celebration of Life of

Dr. Lucille Banks Robinson Miller

Homecoming Service
August 1, 1998
10:00A.M.

Greater Mt. Calvary Holy Church
610 Rhode Island Avenue. N.E.
Washington, District of Columbia

Bishop Alfred Owens - Pastor • Honorable Walter E. Fauntroy - Eulogist • Queen Esther White Young - Officiating

Cover of Lucille's funeral service bulletin

Tom's father, Thomas H. Tipton Sr., was a kind and good man who never remarried after his few years with Tom's mother. He was born in Brookhaven, Mississippi, and in order to escape the lynchings that were so prevalent in the 1940s, he lied about his age, fourteen, telling the Navy recruiter that he was sixteen.

In the Navy he was a mess cook. Following the Navy, he moved to Washington, DC, where he became a janitor at the Department of Commerce and eventually became the chief custodian, supervising over 300 people. Tom Tipton Sr. sang in the choir of the Galbraith AME Zion Church on 6th Street in DC as a baritone, with a style that Tom Jr. sought to emulate. In his obituary from the *Washington Post,* he is remembered briefly and simply as one who "lived a beautiful life." "I questioned God when my father died," said Tom. "He didn't deserve to die. I saw these winos and bootleggers hanging around the corners in Washington, and they were still alive . . . My father was dead. It did not seem fair." Tom's father never saw him play a game of basketball at college, nor did he live long enough to encourage Tom in his singing. He died of cancer at the age of fifty-one, when Tom was only eighteen years old.

As a child, Tom Tipton was immersed in gospel music. "The hymns were my release," said Tom. "They gave me great joy. While I lived with my mother, who was directing choirs all over Washington, DC, I was in church four nights each and every week." Tom credits Reverend R. P. Gainey, pastor of the Corinthian Baptist Church in Washington, DC, who recognized and encouraged Tom's talents at an early age. "I loved the camaraderie of kids singing together," said Tom. "At twelve years old at Grimke Elementary School, I was a soprano and directed the choir. My love of music increased when, as a boy, I broke my leg and was forced to lie down on the sofa of my mother's music school at 1603 S Street. I would lay there with my leg in a cast and listen to the music and my mother's teaching. As my own voice developed, I soon recognized that I was a combination of both my father—I remember seeing him with his chin down, reaching deep to bring out such a beautiful sound—and my mother, who sang soprano."

Tom had many relatives on both sides of the family. Edward Lambert, Tom's great-grandfather and father of Mary Lewis, Tom's grandmother on his mother's side, was the child of slaves. He lived in Orange, Virginia, where Tom and his family visited twice a year. "Orange was a very segregated town," Tom recalled, "but my great-grandfather got along . . . he just got along." Edward owned a grocery store, and Tom could remember his great-grandfather letting him work the cash register. "It was bigger than me!" Tom recalled. "My first sale was a big pretzel, which sold for a penny. At seven years old, it took all of my strength to lean down on the register to make it open so that I could deposit that penny!" At the time of his death, Edward Lambert gave Tom a sword from the Civil War. Tom was eleven years old.

A sad truth of American history, and one that is rarely mentioned, is the exodus from this country of many African-Americans who did not want to live here because of the racism and the discrimination. One of Edward's sons, Tom's great-uncle Raleigh, moved to Rio de Janeiro, Brazil at a young age to escape segregated America. Tom visited his great-uncle twice in Rio, where Raleigh Lambert became the vice-president of a telephone company.

Tom's uncle Nathaniel Tipton lived in New Orleans. It was on one of the family visits there that Tom experienced discrimination. He boarded a bus to go to the movie theater, and there was a sign saying that all persons of color must sit in the back of the bus. "When I arrived at the theater," said Tom, "the ticket cashier took my money and said, 'Boy, you will have to sit upstairs.'" Tom climbed the stairs to the balcony and looked down on a screen that was so small he could barely see the movie. "This was the first time," Tom recalled, "that I can remember seeing a sign on a bus that said, 'Colored People Sit in the Back,' and at a movie theater, 'Colored People Sit In The Balcony.'"

A key influence in Tom's life was his grandfather Edward Lewis, who Tom calls "a saint." He taught Tom the fine points of service and humility. He first was a waiter at the Hamilton Hotel and then a head waiter at Indian Springs Country Club and Manor Country Club in suburban DC. When Tom was just a young boy, Edward would call on Tom to help him. "When I began," said Tom, "his advice was 'Watch me. Watch how I do it, and watch how these people reward me for good service.' Pretty soon I was carrying sixteen covered plates on a tray to the tables."

Edward Lewis - Tom's grandfather

People loved Tom's grandfather, and he was very good to Tom. "He taught me politeness. He showed me how to be courteous. It was ingrained into his personality, into his character. He taught me that the two most important words in the English language are 'thank you.' And so I had this great advantage over other children my age, because they never saw any of this."

"I had five incredible aunts" said Tom, "Elizabeth, Virginia, Esther, Thelma, and Hilda." Hilda was only nine years older than Tom, and all five of them were younger than their big sister, Lucille, Tom's mother. All of them have passed away, the most recently Aunt Hilda in 2013. They all had a role in raising Tom however he was fondest of his Aunt Thelma. She helped Tom with math and also helped him get a job in the early years at the Milton S. Kronheim Company, the largest alcohol distributor in DC. That job allowed him to raise a family and make a good living. It was also Thelma who introduced Tom to his father. "When I was five years old," said Tom, "she took me to my father's house on Christmas Day. Aunt Thelma continued to have a good relationship with my father after my parent's divorce. This was the first time that I can remember seeing my father." There, in the living room of his father's house, next to the tree, was a brand-new red-and-white Schwinn bicycle. Any young boy who can remember back to age five can imagine the thrill of what it was like to see that new bicycle. For Tom, he not only received the gift of a new bike—he received the gift of a father, as well.

1935

Tom seated with aunts Thelma and Hilda
Standing L to R: Virginia, Lucille, Elizabeth and Esther

There were other Christmas days that were memorable for other reasons. At the beginning of his CD "Christmas Eve," Tom tells the story of Christmas 1944, when he was eleven years old. Tom and his mother lived in a one-and-a-half room apartment on Connecticut Avenue in Washington. They were so poor they didn't have a Christmas tree or presents. All they had was each other. Tom's mother was embarrassed, but at the time she could not do anything about the situation. On Christmas Eve, after his mother was asleep, Tom sneaked out of the house and went across the street to the Safeway Store, where they had thrown out a lot of their Christmas decorations that were broken, as well as some Christmas trees that were not purchased earlier in the season. Tom looked through the garbage and found some bulbs that were not broken and some tinsel, as well as a tree that no one else wanted. Tom took these decorations and the tree back across the street and decorated the front room of their apartment. On Christmas morning, when his mother awakened and walked down the short hallway from her bedroom to the front room, she saw the tree and broke down crying. With tears rolling down her cheeks, she took Tom in her arms and held him for a long time. And now, every year when Tom goes to church and they sing his mother's favorite Christmas hymn, "Silent Night," his mind and heart reflect not only on the night the Christ Child was born, but also on that night in 1944, when Tom, on his own, decorated the apartment that he and his mother shared with discarded Christmas decorations from the Safeway across the street from where he lived. For Tom and his mother, as poor as they were, it was the most memorable Christmas ever.

Tom at age 10 with Lucille

Tom lived with his mother through junior high school. She was not one to show much affection or encouragement to her son, which is why Christmas morning of 1944 was so memorable. It was left to his Aunt Thelma to give young Tom the love and nurturing that he needed. Tom can remember at least two times they were put out on the street while he lived with his mother. "She put the buying of her gowns before the paying of the rent! When the landlord would come for the rent, my mother would say to me,

'Go downstairs and tell the man that I am not here.' And I did." In characteristic Tipton optimism, he concludes this story by putting the emphasis on the positive: "But we survived and we came back out on top.

"In my childhood I couldn't go to certain places to eat or to sleep . . . I couldn't even go to the zoo except on certain days. It wasn't right, but we didn't think about it," Tom reflected. "I had the love of God in me, and God knew that I could run a little bit, and God knew that I could shoot a basketball a little bit, and so I believe that was God's way of making up for what I didn't have. God said, 'Well, you can't go here or there, but I'll give you this because you are going to need it someday when you can't afford to pay for your own college education. I'll give you legs to run and I'll give you an eye to shoot a ball, and I'll make you good enough that you can even play against the great Elgin Baylor.'" (Tom played against him on the outdoor courts of Banneker Junior High School.) "What I learned as a child is that God is an equal opportunity employer, so that what I did not have at one stage of my life because of the senselessness of segregation, God made it up to me when I went to college. To this day I don't understand why I didn't have more pain and anger like a lot of my brothers who ended up in jail. But Christ was in my life."

At the age of fifteen, Tom went to live with his father for three years until after he had graduated from high school. They were good years, as Tom found his focus shifting from music to basketball. His mother Lucille was starting another family with the arrival of Tom's two half-brothers Arthur and then Reginald Robinson. Both still live in DC area.

The Neighborhood of Northwest DC

"My neighborhood was mostly all African-American, and I had a lot of friends, including a German boy named Ludvig," said Tom. Tom's life was built around Dunbar and Armstrong high schools and the Lincoln, Republic, and Booker T. theaters. "I knew everyone in my neighborhood, and everyone knew me."

Tom grew up listening to many black preachers, but there was one who stood out. Daddy Grace was a black preacher whose church was at 7th and T Street, across from the Dunbar Theater and just around the corner from Cleveland Elementary where Tom went to school. Daddy Grace opened many churches that he called "houses of prayer," which have continued to thrive even after his death, mixing an "other-world theology" with a "present-world practicality."

"At Christmastime we would go to Daddy, and he would give us gifts," said Tom. "Any day of the week, we could go to Daddy Grace's for lunch or dinner for twenty-five cents, and if you didn't have it, you could get a meal for free.

"Daddy Grace was regarded as a prophet," recalled Tom. "He could preach. And when I say he can preach, I mean it. I don't say that about very many preachers." Daddy Grace had apartment buildings for senior citizens, and would fill as many needs in the black community as he could. Said Tom, "He took care of people . . . I have no problem with Daddy Grace . . . He gave back to the community. When Daddy Grace came to church on Sunday with his Caucasian wife, which was new for my eyes, the ushers would roll out a carpet from his car to the door so that his feet would not touch the sidewalk." One of Daddy Grace's annual fundraising events included putting a floor-to-ceiling Christmas tree in the church sanctuary. The affluent black church members would clip money to the tree and "cover it," said Tom. The cash collected would be used throughout the year to help those not so fortunate with food and clothing.

In his *Short History of Black Washington,* Sam Smith writes about education in the neighborhood where Tom lived: "Denied access to white schools, the community created a self-sufficient educational system good enough to attract suburban African-American students as well as teachers from all over the country. And just to the north, Howard University became the intellectual center of black America. You might run into Langston

Hughes, Alain Locke, or Duke Ellington, all of whom made the U Street area their home before moving to New York."

"Growing up," said Tom, "we knew nothing about drugs. We had heard of marijuana, but we had never seen it. My life was about school, church and family . . . and I was always working to make money."

One of Tom's oldest friends from his neighborhood is Salome Burton. Although she was two years ahead of Tom in Dunbar High School, they have known one another for over 60 years. When asked about Tom's best quality, she replied, "His ability to reach out to anybody and everybody. He is an extravert! In the best of ways, Tom is like a spider's web. He is able to pull you in!" She remembered the time that she had broken her leg and Tom took care of her children, Gail and Ardell, for her. Ardell was wheelchair-bound from elementary school until her death at age 52. "I will forever be in his debt for the kindness he showed my kids," she said. Salome continues to be a good friend of Tom's, keeping Tom updated on the happenings of Washington.

During Tom's school years, there were five high schools in Washington—Phelps, Spingarn, Cardoza, Armstrong, and Dunbar. Tom attended Dunbar High School, so named in honor of the poet Paul Laurence Dunbar. It was the nation's first public high school for African-Americans, originally named Preparatory High School for Colored Youth. Dunbar was known as a college prep school and included in its curriculum courses in Latin and Greek. For many years its students outperformed students at Washington's white high schools on standardized tests.

John Hoskins and Hortense Taylor Pace, Tom's junior high school music teachers, instilled in him a sense of musical purpose and classical understanding. Tom sang in the choir. He said, "It was the most amazing choir I have ever heard in my life. We were honored to be the first black choir in 1950 to sing at Constitution Hall." Tom also participated in many musicals like *Down in the Valley* but mostly sang gospel and classical choral music such as Handel's *Messiah*.

Another one of Tom's great joys while at Dunbar was his participation in his high school quartet, which was named the Golden Jubilaires. "I must confess that we were the best gospel quartet in Washington, DC," reflected Tom. "We sang at programs with the Golden Gate Quartet, the Flying Clouds, and the Dixie Hummingbirds. It was a joy."

Tom was a good student, but he was more interested in sports and working to make money. He was also a Cub Scout and Boy Scout. "The Boy Scouts were a family for me," said Tom. "I earned a lot of medals, and my mother always made sure I was kept neat and clean. My Scout uniform was always meticulous, and my shoes were spit-shined." The Boy Scouts kept Tom out of the gangs that formed in his neighborhood. Tom didn't like to fight, and the Scouts became a safe haven for him.

Tom played basketball for three years at Dunbar, under Coach Charlie Williams. His greatest high school sports accomplishment was to score twenty-six points as a senior against their rival, Dunbar High School in Baltimore, Maryland. He graduated high school in 1951, and had the choice of going to Delaware State in Towson, Delaware; Howard University in DC; or Morgan State in Baltimore, Maryland. "I chose Morgan State in Baltimore," said Tom. "Although I loved her dearly, I wanted to get away from my mother and the DC area."

Chapter Two

From College to Capital Caravan

Great is Thy faithfulness!
Great is Thy faithfulness!
Morning by morning new mercies I see;
All I have needed Thy hand hath provided;
Great is Thy faithfulness, Lord unto me!

"Great is Thy Faithfulness"
Text: Thomas Obediah Chisholm, 1866–1960
Music: William M. Runyan, 1870–1957

On His Own: College Life

In the fall of 1951, Tom entered Morgan State College on a full basketball scholarship. For four years of college, Tom paid for nothing except books. As mentioned, he chose Morgan State College, now Morgan State University, to get away from home. In this respect Tom was not unlike many young people who wanted to get away from home after graduation from high school. He didn't move far—from Washington to Baltimore—but it was far enough.

Tom #38 on Morgan State basketball team

Morgan State University was founded in 1867 as a Bible Institute for the Methodist Episcopal Church. Later it expanded its offerings, and by 1895 it was awarding baccalaureate degrees. Over the years, Morgan has become a most prestigious university, with many renowned African-Americans claiming Morgan as their alma mater, including Earl Graves, publisher of Black Enterprise Magazine; Kweisi Mfume, president of the NAACP; Zora Neale Hurston, novelist; and Deniece Williams, R&B and gospel singer. Besides Morgan State's good reputation, Tom was also influenced to go to there by one of the members of the Golden Jubilaires, Samuel Duckmoore. Tom had the honor of preaching and singing at Samuel's funeral in 2005.

Tom majored in English and speech. He said, "I wanted to major in psychology, but I didn't feel like doing all of that reading! I was good in English, and I was president of my drama club and the Scroller Club, a prerequisite to pledging with Kappa Alpha Psi." During his years at Morgan, Tom belonged to the theatrical fraternity, Alpha Psi Omega, and was in two plays, *Antigone* and *Roughshod Up the Mountain*. In *Roughshod,* Tom played the role of a preacher named Joshua P. Amos. "Throughout that play," said Tom, "I preached my heart out!"

In his second year in college, Tom decided to pledge the Kappa Alpha Psi fraternity and became the president of his pledge class.

He quickly became known as "The Monk," a copycat nickname of sorts after a jazz radio DJ in the Baltimore area named the Mad Monk. Roger Kelly was already a fraternity member when Tom pledged, and they became the best of friends. "I lived in the same hall with Tom at Morgan," recalled Kelly, who is now a retired Army colonel. "We would stay up late into the night playing cards together." Tom's fraternity brothers knew how to have a fun time, but they also did some amazing things to help others. To this day, Tom's fraternity class helps young people who are in need of scholarships and encouragement to get an education through Morgan State University's scholarship fund. Kappa Alpha Psi is a college social fraternity that originated at Indiana University in Bloomington, Indiana, in 1911. Although its charter constitution has never contained any clause that either excluded or suggested the exclusion of a man from membership merely because of his color, creed, or national origin, the fraternity has been predominantly comprised of African-American men. The fraternity's motto: "Achievement in Every Field of Human Endeavor."

Morgan State Kappa Alpha Psi pledgers 1952

21

The college Kappas

*Kappa Alpha Psi reunion with Roger Kelly, Charles MacMillan
and Earl Knight*

While at Morgan, Tom started the first radio station on campus under the call letters of WEAA. He was able to attract well-known musicians to campus, such as Miles Davis, Max Roach, and Dizzy Gillespie. In the words of Roger Kelly, "Tom helped all of us learn about jazz." Tom's cousin, Edward Cleveland, said, "He would travel to our home in White Plains, New York, while he was in college. Tom introduced me and my sisters, Jean and Doris, to jazz. He was way ahead of his time."

In addition to his athleticism on the basketball court, Tom had a number of successes in track and field, as well. Tom goes back to Morgan State University every other year for homecoming. During this bi-annual ritual, he connects with his old track buddies: Jimmy Rogers, Jet Johnson, Josh Culbreth, and Ken Kane, who were nicknamed "The Flying Four." Herb Washington was also a regular relay member. They became famous for running the half-mile and mile relays, and it was Josh Culbreth who would become an Olympic bronze medalist in 1956 in Melbourne, Australia, for the 100-yard hurdles. It was Culbreth who taught Tom to run the hurdles.

Morgan State track team 1951

"One of my favorite memories of Josh Culbreth was when I had to sub for Herb Washington and run the first leg of the relay," Tom said. "Josh simply told me, 'Don't fall down, Tom, and act like you can run!'" Their friendships run deep, and each year Tom's relay team travels to Philadelphia for the famous Penn Relays. "We would take a bullet for one another," Tom said. "We are a family. Running the first leg of the 400—and 200-meter relays at Druid Park in 1954 and winning two gold medals is one of the great joys of my life." Also joining the family of lifelong friends from Morgan State is Charles MacMillan, from Chester, Pennsylvania. "Mac" and Tom were college roommates for three of the four years on campus. They shared track and basketball (Mac ran the 440 and was the basketball center) and also "chased a few girls together" during college, according to Tom. Charles also has the entertainment industry bond with Tom, being a career-long business manager for singer Jerry Butler. Tom and Mac still talk weekly.

Track team reunion L to R: Walter Carr, Bill Day, Charles MacMillan, Roger Kelly and Tom

Tom's college years in Baltimore were difficult years for persons of color. They were years when the crust which surrounded the practice of segregation was beginning to break away, but not without a struggle. At the center of the desegregation of Baltimore were many Morgan students, including Tom and Roger Kelly. "We integrated the theaters in Baltimore," recalled Kelly. It was a time of personal growth for Tom, and cultural growth for America.

Life in the Army

Right after graduation from Morgan State College in 1955, Tom Tipton was inducted into the Army. He was sent to Fort Jackson, South Carolina, to a place called Tank Hill. His company was at least two-thirds black, and the other third white. "Basic training was very tough," recalled Tom. "It was also racially separated."

Most of the black recruits were illiterate and from the south. These recruits would awaken Tom in the middle of the night and ask him to read them their letters from home. As for the officers, they were all white, and as Tom remembers, "Most were racist."

As Commander-in-Chief of the Armed Forces, President Harry Truman issued Executive Order 9981 on July 26, 1948. It read: "It is hereby declared to be the policy of the President that there shall be equality of treatment and opportunity for all persons in the armed services without regard to race, color, religion, or national origin. The policy shall be put into effect as rapidly as possible, having due regard to the time required to effectuate any necessary changes without impairing efficiency or morale." It was just a few years after this order that Tom Tipton entered the Army. Needless to say, this executive order was a long way from being universally accepted within the military. In his article "Black-White Relations in the U.S. Military 1940–1972," author Major Alan M. Osur writes: "Significantly, instead of simply permitting the military services to proceed on their own, Truman created the President's Committee on Equality of Treatment and Opportunity in the Armed Forces, commonly called the Fahy Committee after its chairman, Charles Fahy. The Fahy Committee started meeting in January of 1949 and submitted its report, 'Freedom to Serve,' in May of 1950. The report took so long to issue because the committee was an action committee, forcing the services constantly to change and modify their plans and policies to meet the goal of full desegregation. The committee also took time because the Army continually resisted efforts to push it along."

After six weeks of basic training, Tom was at the top of his class, along with twelve others. His captain told the group of thirteen that they had two choices. The first choice was that their service could be extended to a third year, and they would be promoted to Second Lieutenant. The second choice was to go to cryptology school in Georgia. Twelve chose the first choice, and Tom chose the second.

"I was shipped to Augusta, Georgia," reflects Tom. "It was a bad time . . . a bad period in the life of this great country." Tom was the only black man in his company. He was fully aware at this time that there would be attempts to force him out. For recreation, he played basketball, sometimes with Tom Gola, who would later play for the Philadelphia Warriors. One day Tom left practice early and went back to the barracks to rest before dinner. Three sergeants came into the barracks and kicked his bunk over. One of them yelled, "What the hell are you doing in here Tipton?" Upset, but without anger in his voice, Tom replied, "I am waiting for chow." They called him names and told him to leave and report to the First Sergeant. Tom went to the library, put on some headphones, and listened to music by Chuck Berry, Aretha Franklin, and Duke Ellington until it was time to eat. Early the next morning, the same three sergeants entered the barracks and kicked Tom's bunk over, yelling at him, calling him names, and telling him to go to Captain Swedelski's office. The three marched Tom over to see the Captain. Upon arrival, Captain Swedelski asked Tom, "I thought they told you to go and see the First Sergeant yesterday." Tom was silent. The captain was furious, and after about fifteen minutes of name-calling and belittlement, he concluded by saying, "I'll see you in court. You are going to be court-martialed!" Tom walked out the door and went to see a white lieutenant attorney, and a dear friend. The attorney looked at Tom and said, "Tom, this is absolute madness." Tom responded by saying, "But look where we are—Augusta, Georgia!" This was during the time of Jim Crow—if you were black, there were black taxis, black hotels, black grocery stores, and black restrooms. Tom's friend said that he would defend him in the court martial, but Tom said, "I will defend myself!"

The day of the court-martial came, and the courtroom was packed. Tom was asked to share his story, and he did. Tom made his case for twenty-five minutes, noting that although he had been ordered to go and see the First Sergeant, he had not been told *when* to do so. In Tom's words, "They could not believe that this six-foot, four-inch Negro could stand amongst these white people and eloquently defend himself." In the courtroom were thirty to thirty-five sergeants, which, to Tom, looked like a lynch mob. There was also a man in the second row that Tom did not know. Following an hour's recess, court resumed, with the judge asking Tom to stand. "Private First Class Tipton, we find you not guilty." Tom cried and walked out of the courtroom with five white brothers who testified on his behalf. They were all members of Tom's basketball team. Tom's Army experience had left him scarred. "They wanted to ruin my life, send me to jail, and take my reputation away," he said.

Following the court martial trial, Tom was summoned to Colonel Zarr's office. Nervously, he went, and upon entering, saluted him. "I am a big fan of yours," remarked the colonel. "You play quite a good game of basketball." And then the colonel gave him a choice. "Mr. Tipton, you can either be transferred to the Pentagon in Washington, DC, or you can be shipped to Paris." Tom chose to go back home to Washington, where he did cryptology work on the midnight shift at the Pentagon.

And how did he get back to Washington from Augusta, Georgia? The five friends who were on Tom's Army basketball team took up a collection, raised seventy dollars, and bought him a car. Three days later, he was in route from Georgia to Washington and arrived in Richmond, Virginia, where the car broke down. He left it on the side of the road and caught a Greyhound bus for the rest of the journey. In Tom's words, "A new chapter in my life was beginning."

Army buddies L to R: Bob Shuker, Tom and Tom Gola

The Capital Caravan: Music and Family Again

Following his time in the Army, Tom Tipton was back in his home community of Washington, DC. He took and passed the test that would qualify him for any number of excellent jobs in the federal government, but he turned them down. "My aunts thought I was crazy," recalled Tom, "but I wanted something else." That something else was a job in the media, and in particular WUST radio. Tom started a weekend jazz show titled "Jazz Limited" and became the assistant to station manager Bob McEwen. McEwen emceed the first black television show in America on WTTG-TV. "He was a brilliant black man," said Tom, "who knew how to make money." Tom worked with McEwen on the program "Capital Caravan," sponsored by Breath of Pine furniture polish and Bon-Ton potato chips. For the next year, besides his work on radio, Tom was also a substitute fifth grade teacher at Shaw Junior High School and a salesman for the Kirby Vacuum Company. Tom laughingly said, "I sold two—one to my mother, and another to my Aunt Thelma!" Tom was also a disc jockey at record or sock hops (informal dances sponsored by clubs or schools). For this job, Bob McEwen gave

Tom the title of King Hi-Fi. Tom was also working record hops for Tex Gathing, a disc jockey from WOOK in Washington. "I was twenty-eight or twenty-nine years old, and I would go throughout the community spinning records for the kids," recalled Tom. "I tried to teach them some values along with just spinning records." It was through his friendship with Gathing that Tom met such jazz greats as Thelonious Monk, Billy Eckstein, and Dave Brubeck.

King Hi-fi

On Sundays, Tom would travel with his mother, who would always have an engagement at a church or an anniversary party for a pastor. He would sing at least two solos for her, "What a Friend We Have in Jesus" and "His Eye is On The Sparrow," the two standards that are still a part of every Tipton performance. Laughing, Tom said, "We were always paid in cash because you could never trust a check from a minister!"

Tom also had his first experience in the marketing world as a salesman for Hamm's Beer Company and Kronheim Beverage Distributors, becoming the first black salesman hired by Hamm's on the East Coast.

In Washington in 1959, Tom was blessed with his first daughter, Cassandra. Tom was the primary caregiver for Cassandra for her first few months of life, as her birth mother was in a crisis situation and unable to care for her. Tom welcomed the helping hands of his Aunt Virginia. Tom knew he needed to provide a more secure home and family life for his daughter and arranged for her adoption by Ella Walker. Cassandra has thrived and excelled in her life, receiving a college education. She has married and has a successful career as a senior vice president for a Fortune 500 corporation in California. Cassandra and husband Kelvin Pye are the parents of Tom's four grandsons, Richard, William, Steven, and Eric.

Cassandra and Kelvin Pye with Richard, William, Steven and Eric in 1997

In late 1959, it was in a Washington hospital that Tom first became acquainted with Brenda Kellog. "My mother, the diva," Tom said, "would become exhausted, and she would check herself into a hospital for a week or so. She loved all of the nurses checking in on her, and all of the flowers that she received. One day a gorgeous nurse walked in to give my mother a pill. I whispered to my mother, 'I am going to date this lady.'" And Tom did. Tom married Brenda and they had a daughter, Beverly, in March of 1962. "Brenda was a beautiful woman and a wonderful nurse," he said. Tom and Brenda divorced after a couple of years. Brenda passed away a few years ago, suffering from complications of Alzheimer's. Her death was a tremendous blow to Tom. The start of a family again in the 1960s with two lovely and talented daughters has been a source of pride and joy through his adult life. Beverly has also earned a college degree and is employed in Baltimore where she now lives with her husband, Drew Hammond. She is also a gifted minister and singer and performs frequently in the gospel music field.

CHAPTER THREE

A WORLD OF CHANGE

This is the day
That the Lord has made;
Let us rejoice
And be glad in it.

"This is the Day"
Les Garrett
Text: Psalm 118:24

In the summer of 1963, Martin Luther King Jr. came to Washington, DC. He was there to organize the now famous March on Washington that culminated in him delivering his "I Have A Dream" speech on the steps of the Lincoln Memorial on August 28, 1963. This was a year that was marked by racial unrest and civil rights demonstrations. Attack dogs and fire hoses were turned on demonstrators in Birmingham, Alabama, and King was arrested. It was while he was under arrest in Birmingham that he wrote "Letter from Birmingham Jail," in which he advocated civil disobedience against unjust laws. That summer, the Civil Rights Act was stalled in Congress, and everyone was tense. Many news sources reported that since President John F. Kennedy was unable to convince King and the other civil rights leaders to call off the March on Washington, he publicly announced his support on July 17. He was concerned mostly with the potential of violence occurring.

Tom Tipton was working at the all-black station WUST when King arrived for an interview and for an appearance on Tom's mother's gospel music program. "My mother introduced me to Dr. King, and he invited me to join him and others at the Dunbar Hotel that evening," said Tom. He went to the hotel that night, the first black-owned hotel in Washington, and it was there that he sat in on the planning for the march. "In the early planning stages, those around Dr. King were trying to help him with what he would talk about in his speech," said Tom. "I wasn't there for that discussion, but my mother was. My mother was a close friend of Mahalia Jackson. It was Mahalia who said, 'Martin, why don't you tell them about your dream?' Dr. King had been talking about this dream that he had concerning how we should all come together— black folk and white folk. Of course this speech is now considered by some as the greatest of the twentieth century. I don't think it was, but that is a matter of personal preference. I believe that his best speech was the 'Mountaintop Speech' he gave in Memphis, when he knew that his time on this earth was almost up."

In Washington, Tom, along with Dunbar classmate Walter Fauntroy, helped the march leaders to galvanize all of the churches and synagogues for the march. "There were meetings with the black leaders in the Jewish synagogues, and Methodists were meeting with Roman Catholics. It was huge!" Tom recalled. During the march, it was Tom's responsibility to make sure there were portable public toilets available along the route.

It is easy to forget the concern and downright fear that many had about the "March on Washington and how it could have erupted into rioting. Tom said, "There was something spiritual about the preparation for the march . . . I felt calm and assured that with Dr. King as the leader, there would not be any trouble. Also keeping things calm was the participation of so many white churches. It was like the time had come at this specific time for a peaceful march of grievance. Many things could have gone wrong, but they didn't. If you ask me what the most amazing thing that happened in that March on Washington, I would say that there was peace. At the March, there were 250,000 people, but amazingly no one was locked up and nobody went to jail. We prayed a lot and hugged a lot."

During Dr. King's "I Have A Dream" speech at the Lincoln Memorial, Tom was standing in about the fourth row back with

Jim Hawks from WUST radio. "I was looking up," recalled Tom, "and the Nation of Islam was around him . . . it was a beautiful day! Martin Luther King Jr. was surrounded on the stage by members of the Islam community not as guards, but as a sign of strength, unity, and support for equal black opportunities of all religious groups. Many people were expecting trouble to break out, but it didn't. The Holy Spirit was surrounding us." Tom was not very impressed with the beginning of Dr. King's speech. "He started out slow. But then as he approached the 'I have a dream' segment, the spirit of the Baptist preacher came out. The Holy Spirit took over." It was at that point that Dr. King connected with what Mahalia Jackson had told him: "Tell them about your dream, Martin." And he did, and everyone became caught up in the wave that King and the Holy Spirit had started. "White and black," said Tom, "the Spirit caught everybody—even those who did not understand what the Holy Spirit is—it hit them! The whole place just vibrated. It hit me and went all of the way back to the Washington Monument."

At the time, Tom Tipton was not aware of the historical significance of what he was witnessing. He knew, however, that something was changing. He felt something was happening—he felt different. Everybody felt different, and everybody felt good. He didn't know what it was. He felt like shouting, but he didn't know why. Dr. King had preached a sermon like Tom expected to receive in the Baptist Church almost every Sunday. "A good minister will take you to a place where you are dancing on the ceiling!" said Tom. It was only when the media began to talk and write about the powerful words spoken at the Lincoln Memorial that day in August of 1963 that Tom began to realize how special it was. "I thought to myself, 'I was a part of it.' I brought the chicken—my mother had concessions of fried chicken, potato salad, and bread for $1.50. I drove a bus, I held the babies in the nursery, I helped an elderly woman up off of the ground where she had fainted. We became proud! There was no looting or stealing, or fights. And it drifted across the nation from the Lincoln Memorial—across the North and the South and into the White

House. This one man, Dr. King, who had been to the mountaintop, who knew one day that he would be assassinated for his beliefs and his leadership in those beliefs, brought us all together."

Tom Tipton singing at an event to honor corporate sponsors who assisted in funding the building of the Martin Luther King Jr Memorial in Washington DC

The words that touched Tom Tipton and the world so profoundly are from Martin Luther King Jr. on that August 28, 1963, afternoon:

I am happy to join with you today in what will go down in history as the greatest demonstration for freedom in the history of our nation . . .

I say to you today, my friends, that in spite of the difficulties and frustrations of the moment, I still have a dream. It is a dream deeply rooted in the American dream.

I have a dream that one day this nation will rise up and live out the true meaning of its creed: "We hold these truths to be self-evident: that all men are created equal." . . .

And then with the stirring spiritual passion for which he was known, Dr. King concluded:

Let freedom ring from the snowcapped Rockies of Colorado!

Let freedom ring from the curvaceous slopes of California!

But not only that; let freedom ring from Stone Mountain of Georgia!

Let freedom ring from Lookout Mountain of Tennessee!

Let freedom ring from every hill and molehill of Mississippi. From every mountainside, let freedom ring.

And when this happens, when we allow freedom to ring, when we let it ring from every village and every hamlet, from every state and every city, we will be able to speed up that day when all of God's children, black men and white men, Jews and Gentiles, Protestants and Catholics, will be able to join hands and sing in the words of the old Negro spiritual, "Free at last! Free at last! Thank God Almighty, we are free at last!"

"The world was changed after Dr. King spoke at the Lincoln Memorial," reflected Tom. "Even those who disliked his vision respected him as a human being. Even in the South, where they still call him some very nasty names—even in the South they respected him. He changed the mood of the people, and he was able to get the media behind him. When Dr. King traveled, his rooms would be wiretapped. He had enemies who were always trying to get something on him. There were threats on his life. He knew this. He also knew his life would end as a result of his efforts. But he kept his focus on the larger picture, on the greater good that he was trying to accomplish. Dr. King made us better than we had been."

CHAPTER FOUR

ADVANCE MAN AND BUSINESS OWNER

I don't worry o'er the future,
For I know what Jesus said,
And today I'll walk beside him,
For He knows what is ahead.

"I Know Who Holds Tomorrow"
Composer: Ira F. Stanphill
1950

In 1968, Tom Tipton was the president of the black chapter of the Young Democrats in Washington. He was invited to the Sheraton Hotel in Washington to be present for the announcement by Vice President Hubert Humphrey that he was going to run for President. At the announcement were some representatives from the Minnesota Opportunities Industrialization Center (OIC) that Humphrey had helped to get started. Following the announcement, they asked Tom if he could take them to get some soul food . . . Tom agreed and took them downtown to the 7th Street Grill. "We had some chitlins (pig intestines) and collard greens, black-eyed peas, and potato salad. And they were just as happy as they could be." Tom invited the group back to his house, where they listened to music. One of the Young Democrats, Stanley King, wanted to make a phone call, and so Tom told him he could do so in his office upstairs. As Tom recalled, "Stanley went upstairs, and in a few moments he came running back downstairs saying, 'Hey Joe (Buckoften), this brother'—pointing at me—'is in public relations! We need you in Minnesota!'" At the time, Tom was doing very well in Washington. He still had his Sunday jazz show on the radio, and his quartet was singing all over the area. "I was just fine," said Tom. "I had no intention of moving anywhere, especially somewhere cold!"

After considerable conversation, Tom persisted with his "no, thank you." "But then they got slick on me," Tom laughed. "They went to Hubert Humphrey and Cecil Newman, who was at that time Humphrey's number-one representative in the African-American community." Hubert Humphrey told Tom to "buy a pair of long-underwear and come to Minnesota anyway!"

"Cecil Newman called me from Minnesota and said, 'Tom would you consider coming out to Minnesota to look at what we are doing?'" Tom insisted again, "Mr. Newman, with all due respect, I am not interested." Finally, Stanley King, who first suggested that Tom come to Minnesota, called him. Tom recalled, "Stanley was a smooth-talking preacher, and he finally convinced me to come to Minnesota to see what they were doing."

Once in Minnesota, Tom was wined and dined and received a full tour of the Opportunities Industrialization Center. He thanked them for their hospitality and returned to his life in Washington. In April of 1968, Dr. Martin Luther King Jr. was murdered in Memphis, and then in July, Senator Robert Kennedy was killed in Los Angeles. "I was on the couch recovering from back surgery, watching the returns from the California Democratic Primary," recalled Tom, "and then it happened. Bobby Kennedy was shot. It was around one o'clock in the morning in Washington, DC. I saw the whole thing. And the Holy Spirit came over me . . . Now, I don't know much about the Holy Spirit, but people have told me that I have the Spirit in me, and I certainly felt it that night." Tom's back problems prevented him from getting on his knees, and so he looked up and said, "'Okay, Lord. You are speaking to me.' And he said, 'You need to go to Minnesota and serve.'" This was a pivotal, teachable moment in Tom's life. He was beginning to understand that he was placed on this earth to serve others.

Tom moved to Minnesota in the fall of 1968 and went to work for the Opportunities Industrialization Center as public relations director and fundraiser. The OIC was a training center where people could learn basic skills in reading, writing, printing, and welding, and it was in its infant stage when Tom was working there. It has since become an organization with forty-four affiliates in twenty-two states. It was founded by Reverend Leon Sullivan in 1964, in an abandoned jailhouse in Philadelphia. It serves the poor, unemployed, underemployed, youth, and families. Tom's fraternity brothers made a bet that he would not last more than a year in cold Minnesota. They were wrong; Tom stayed at OIC until 1970 and in Minnesota until 1979. At the time, however, Tom also thought that he would only be in Minnesota for a year. "I was only going to be away from Washington a short time, because I was going to return and run for Congress against my high school classmate, Walter Fauntroy . . . And I think I would have beaten him because my mother had a lock on all of the black churches in DC, and both Walter and I had gone to Dunbar High School.

"Coming to Minnesota was culture shock for me." said Tom. "I would walk down the street and people would say 'good morning' to me. One morning I walked into Dayton's Department Store in downtown Minneapolis to buy my mother a small gift. My brother was with me, and when we purchased the gift, my brother took out nine pieces of identification! The woman behind the counter said, 'Mister, you don't need to do that. You just need one piece of identification.'" When they walked out of the store, Tom's brother said to him, "These people are crazy. They just want one piece of ID!"

And so Tom stayed through the first year—a difficult year. It was 1968, and after the death of Martin Luther King Jr. cities were being set on fire during riots that summer, including areas of Minneapolis.

To set the tone of Tom's new job at the OIC, he shared this story: "On my first day as the public relations director at OIC, the phone rings. It is Dayton's Department Store calling to say that they had a student of OIC in the credit department, and the student had left her baby. She couldn't pay her bill, and so she left her baby as payment! This was my first day! And so I thought, 'This is really bad. Everybody is going to lose . . . OIC is going to lose, and Dayton's is going to lose." Two nights before his first day on the job, Tom went to a press party downtown and met some people from the media, including one person from WCCO television named Tom Cousins. "I knew one person at WCCO from that party, and they were getting ready to break the story about the baby being left at Dayton's," Tom said. "I called WCCO—Tom Cousins—and said, 'I have a problem. I can't have bad press about this situation, and I need your help.' WCCO agreed to wait on the story, and I went to Dayton's to talk with Earl Brooks, who was their vice president. While there, I talked to the media, and I took the baby and the mother from the store and brought them back to OIC. Earl Brooks writes a check out of his pocket, not from Dayton's, to pay the bill. The story is non-published, and OIC and Dayton's are saved from some very bad publicity."

While working at the OIC, Tom was also working for Hubert Humphrey's election team. He was what was called an advance man. He would help arrange for people in the campaign to speak at various venues. But his relationship with Humphrey was more than just political; it was spiritual. "He could have been a Baptist preacher," said Tom of Humphrey. "He was filled with a spirituality and emotion, as well as an intellect that made you feel that he was one of your own. He could go into any black church and do as well as any black pastor I had ever met, and I have met a lot of them! Many politicians are not sincere when they visit black neighborhoods or churches, but Hubert Humphrey could come and was welcomed to stay all day. That appealed to me. It was natural for him. How it was natural for him, I do not know.

"Hubert and Muriel Humphrey were from South Dakota. They had never lived side by side with black people. Together they traveled to New Orleans and saw some of the worst poverty in our country. Muriel said, 'We cannot have this in our America.' This was before the 1948 Democratic Convention. Hubert and Muriel made up their minds that something had to be done about this."

In a renowned 1948 speech before the Democratic National Convention in Philadelphia Hubert Humphrey took his public stand demanding civil rights for racial minorities. At the time, Humphrey was the mayor of Minneapolis and a rising star in Democratic politics. Given a place to speak at the convention, Humphrey used this national podium to decry the terrible conditions of black America and encouraged his party to abandon its racist Jim Crow laws in the South, which mandated racial segregation in all public facilities for black Americans. It was a courageous speech and one that moved the Democratic Party to the forefront of civil rights, beginning the decline of the party's influence in the South. In part, Humphrey said,

> *Friends, delegates, I do not believe that there can be any compromise on the guarantees of the civil rights which we have mentioned in the minority report (the minority report from the Democratic Party platform). In spite of my desire to see everybody here in honest and unanimous agreement, there are some matters which I think must be stated clearly and without qualification. There can be no hedging . . . There will be no hedging, and there will be no watering down—if you please—of the instruments and principles of the civil rights program.*
>
> *My friends, to those who say that we are rushing this issue of civil rights, I say to them we are 172 years late.*

Following the convention, enraged southern Democrats formed the Dixiecrat Party, nominating Strom Thurmond from South Carolina as their own presidential candidate. Their plan to pull southern support from the Democrats and defeat Truman and his pro-civil rights agenda backfired. Harry Truman won a stunning upset victory over his Republican opponent, Thomas E. Dewey, and was elected President.

What was it in Hubert Humphrey that made him such an advocate of civil rights? Certainly the experience he and Muriel had in New Orleans was a catalyst, but what was it within him that made him such a spokesperson for equality of the races? Generalizing, Tom believes that it came from his Midwestern personality, a personality that Midwesterners often take for granted. "Midwesterners are real and caring people," said Tom. "West Coast is celebrityville, a show, and a lot of the East Coast is simply too busy. It is 'What can you do for me?' The Midwest is very simple . . . people care. Why do they care? I don't know. They just do. It is their way. It's in their nature." For Tom and for millions of others, Hubert Humphrey was the embodiment of this Midwestern caring attitude. "Humphrey was the first person I ever met who never saw any color. He just never saw it," recalled Tom. "Muriel was the same way."

Working a convention with Hubert Humphrey

Skip Humphrey, the former attorney general for the State of Minnesota and Hubert and Muriel's son, said of Tom's relationship with his father, "Tom was a real, true friend. He was a member of Dad's inner core. They were very, very close. Tom was the kind of guy that Dad could bounce ideas off of. You could let all pretense down with Tom, and in politics this is very important. There was a depth of relationship that Dad had with Tom that he highly cherished."

In 1968 Humphrey was defeated in his bid for President of the United States by Richard Nixon.

***A gathering with Hubert Humphrey and Salome Burton
in Waverly, Minnesota***

From 1968 to 1970, Tom raised money for the OIC in Minneapolis and helped with the Humphrey campaign. But money for the OIC was always uncertain. "Half the time we didn't get paid," recalled Tom. "The program was just getting off of the ground, and money was always a problem." Eventually, with the help of Hubert Humphrey, the center saw success and the staff grew from ten employees to fifty-five. It began to make a real difference in the lives of thousands of people.

Tom put his musical talents and connections to work. He put on a show at the Guthrie Theater in Minneapolis that raised $25,000 for the OIC. He performed two concerts at Orchestra Hall, raising $30,000 each, with special guests like Harry Belafonte. His mother traveled to Minnesota to attend one of the Orchestra Hall concerts.

Orchestra Hall concert V.I.P.s Stanley King, Harry Belafonte and Tom.

Tom continued on in Minneapolis, doing six television specials for WCCO TV titled "Black Sounds of Our Time." His good friend, Mahalia Jackson, was one of his guests, as well as Doris Hines and Hubert Humphrey.

Tom's guest Gov. Wendell Anderson on another
WCCO production Talk In

During his work with the OIC, Tom met many people with whom he formed lifelong friendships. Tom sang the National Anthem at Minnesota Vikings games nineteen times over the years at both the Metropolitan Stadium and the Hubert H. Humphrey Metrodome. This led to his friendships with many Minnesota Vikings players, including Jim Marshall, Alan Page, and Carl Eller. In 1969 he met Willie and Jeanne (Arland) Peterson. Willie played the organ for the Minnesota Twins in the Met Stadium, and Jeanne continued in the role after his passing. Tom and Jeanne also maintained their friendship as

Jeanne worked performances for twenty years with WCCO TV playing jazz piano and singing. Throughout the years Tom has stayed connected with this top jazz family of Minnesota, watching the family grow with the addition of the musically gifted Peterson children: Billy, Ricky, Patty, Paul, and Linda, and now third generation musicians as well.

At one OIC gathering at Jim Marshall's home, Tom met jazz pianist Billy Wallace. "Billy is one of the greatest jazz players of all time," Tom said. "He touched my life through jazz . . . He is God-sent and is one of my closest friends." In addition to singing with Billy's trio at the St. Paul Hilton, Tom and Billy collaborated on many music performances, including Tom's first album, a jazz album called "Tommy Tipton: Full of Song," recorded in 1969. The album, recorded and produced by UA Recording Corporation, was copyrighted with DBT Records, 2434 Clinton Ave. in Minneapolis, Minnesota. Title tracks included "I Could Write a Book," "By the Time I Get to Phoenix," "Here's That Rainy Day," "Night Song," "Little Girl Blue," "God Bless the Child," "I'll Be Darned Dear," "Old Folks," "Nobody Knows," and "Imagination." All arrangements were by Billy Wallace, who also played piano on the album. Other album musicians included Jim Marentic on bass, Jack Bertelsen on drums, and Mike Elliott on guitar.

Recording session for Tommy Tipton: Full of Song

Switching roles with pianist Billy Wallace

In 1969 Tom also recorded his album "Tom Tipton: Hymns My Mother Taught Me" in Washington with Billy Wallace at the piano. "My mother didn't know I recorded it or that it was named after her. She was totally shocked when I gave it to her," said Tom. "I do remember that we only had four hours of studio time and that Billy and I made only one recording of each track. That was a pretty challenging task and the fastest album compilation I have ever done." Songs on this recording were "He Knows Just How Much We Can Bear," "His Eye is on the Sparrow," "I Believe," "Precious Lord," "Only Believe," "The Old Rugged Cross," "He'll Understand," "Sometimes I Feel Like a Motherless Child," "Move Me," "Something Within," and "Battle Hymn of the Republic."

Hymns My Mother Taught Me

A year later, Tom recorded a CD in honor of his father, "Tom Tipton Sings the Old Hymns." Little detail is known about this recording. Songs include "Knock and the Door Shall be Opened," "Sweet Hour of Prayer," "It is Well With My Soul," "Count Your Blessings," "In the Garden," "Holy, Holy, Holy," "Down by the

Riverside," "What a Friend We Have in Jesus," "Nobody Knows the Trouble I've Seen," "Come Ye Disconsolate," and "He."

Tom Tipton Sings the Old Hymns

Tom also contributed his vocals to the jazz CD recording of Billy Wallace in 1979 called "Coming Home."

Business Owner

In 1970, Stanley King, the director of the Opportunities Industrialization Center, resigned. King asked Tom if he would like to become director, to which Tom replied, "Stanley, I did not come to Minnesota to be the director of OIC!" With Stanley King leaving, Tom felt it was his time to leave, as well.

. . . with love, from the people behind you at Vanguard

Dear Tom,

We're used to writing ads . . . not testimonials. We can dash out sayings like "new & improved" or "big tastin' biscuit", but have trouble expressing our thoughts of you. You're a beautiful person . . . a warm and talented human being. If somebody could mass produce Tom Tiptons, we'd have one heck of a product to sell. Until then, thanks for being the one and only you.

A page from TCOIC's Honors Event

When Tom Tipton left
our firm, he had
five letters of recommendation:

Tom Tipton is one of many successful Minnesotans who
began their careers, either as employees or trainees, at the
Twin Cities Opportunities Industrialization Center. We at
TCOIC are proud of Tom and of all the other TCOIC
alumni who have moved on to bigger and better things. After
all, that's what TCOIC is — a springboard for people.

WE HELP OURSELVES · **TWIN CITIES OPPORTUNITIES INDUSTRIALIZATION CENTER INC.**

TCOIC · 834 N. 7TH STREET / MINNEAPOLIS, MINNESOTA 55411 / 339-7621

CHAIRMAN OF THE BOARD
John F. Bolger

EXECUTIVE DIRECTOR
Frederick D. Felder, Jr.

TCOIC Message

"I asked the Lord, 'Okay, Lord, I am here, here in Minnesota. What do you want to do with me?'" Tom thought that he wanted to open a soul food restaurant, but in the end he began an advertising agency that he called Vanguard. Tom found a great deal of inspiration from H. Naylor Fitzhugh. He was the department head of marketing at Howard University and a Dunbar High School graduate. He taught marketing and business management for thirty-one years and owned a consulting firm. Tom was touched by his knowledge of the world and of marketing and his love of people and family. Tom opened his business in September of 1970 in downtown Minneapolis at 1111 Nicollet Mall, which was soon to become home to the present Orchestra Hall, which opened in 1974. The business was then relocated to 15 South 9th Street. When asked why the name Vanguard, Tom replied, "I just wanted a name that sounded strong. The Vanguard Agency was the first and only black-run advertising agency at that time in Minnesota." Tom owes much of the credit for Vanguard's success to the love and support of Eula and James "Bud" Ward. He provided the hands-on training from his business in Washington. He taught Tom everything he could about marketing. It was Bud who outlined the business plan and helped with the media direction when Vanguard sought the Land O'Lakes account. Through his contacts with the Urban Coalition and work at the OIC, Tom met many CEOs who served as tremendous resources to him as he set up his agency. It was at this point in Tom's journey that guiding support came from the likes of Wheelock Whitney Jr., George Masko, and the late Jim Binger—one of the most dominant forces in the Minnesota world of business.

Tom and George Masko in 2008

Pillsbury inspiration

In commenting about Vanguard, Tom said, "I had to show that the black market was not some kind of philosophical or mythical attitude. My competitors were the best agencies out there. So, when it came to knowing what dictated the buying habits of 25 million people, I wanted my clients to know there was no place else to go to get the job done."

When you're hungry and in a rush...

Get a five-pack from Hungry Jack®

When five biscuits are enough, get a little can of Hungry Jack® Biscuits. They come five in a can for your convenience and you'll find them in the refrigerator case at your grocery store. Some people call them, "five Jacks in a pack," but, whatever you call them, they are five big, fluffy, buttermilk biscuits. And they're always fresh. So, for breakfast, lunch or supper, or anytime you get hungry, break open that five pack and slip them in the oven for about ten minutes.

They're GOOD! They're Hungry Jack® biscuits.

Hungry Pillsbury **Jack**
BISCUITS

A Vanguard-created advertisement

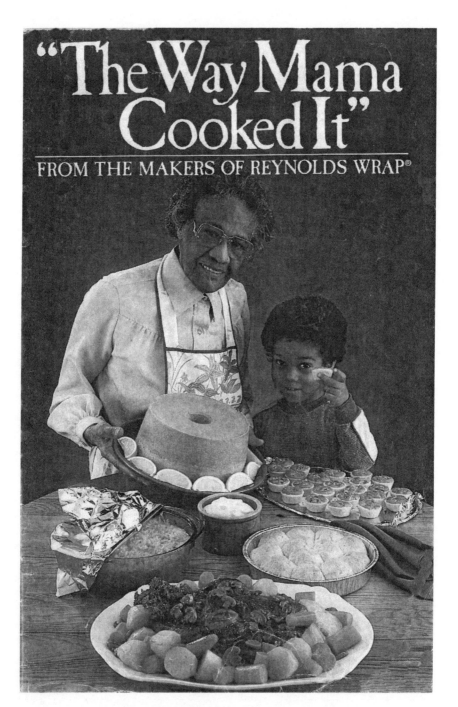

Vanguard advertising included a cookbook

Settling into life in Minnesota, Tom purchased a home in St. Louis Park. He also had a boat on Lake Minnetonka. His work kept him with little extra time, but when time allowed, he enjoyed being out on the water and socializing with friends. Tom made many appearances at the Sabathani Baptist Church, often singing with the choir. Their pianist, Bill Perry, was Tom's accompanist for many events in years to come. Bill's music and voice will always be a part of Tom. Tom met an energetic eighteen-year-old girl named Debbie on the campaign trail for Hubert Humphrey. Tom had been asked by her mother to keep her safe on a campaign trip to Florida. That Humphrey faithful campaigner has been a friend of Tom's for more than forty years. Now Debbie Estes and her husband Ralph continue to support Tom and his music. The couple has entertained Tom and his music family through the years. Debbie was instrumental in planning Tom's seventy-fifth birthday celebration gala. She continues to keep Tom apprised of political happenings in the state and country and promotes and supports his performance appearances.

Tom had many business contacts, including Hubert Humphrey. As he began the Vanguard agency, Tom also began to work for the 1972 Humphrey Presidential Campaign. Since 1968, Tom had become very close to the Humphreys, who trusted him as an advisor and organizer for the campaign. "I was one of the top leaders in the campaign," recalled Tom. "I was in charge of the black vote nationwide. I arranged for the Humphreys to speak in black churches all over the country."

There was one particular event where Tom surprised Hubert. Tom had arranged for the senator to speak at the Metropolitan Baptist Church in Washington, the largest black church in the nation's capital. Before Humphrey spoke, the pastor asked Tom if he would sing a song. "I knew a lot of black ministers because my mother was still the number-one black voice on gospel radio," Tom said. "Everyone knew her, and so they knew her son." When Tom walked past Humphrey on his way to the microphone, the senator looked at Tom very strangely. "Hubert was aware of my political work and my time in radio and television, but he never knew that

I could sing," Tom said. "When I finished and walked back to my seat, Hubert said to me, 'Tom, I didn't know that you could sing like that!'" Tom replied, "You never asked!" From that time forward, whenever Tom traveled with Hubert Humphrey, he would always sing.

The 1972 Hubert Humphrey Presidential Campaign took Tom away from his business, which almost killed the business. In Tom's words, "The business was going to Hell!" It was early in the morning in Cleveland, Ohio, that Tom was summoned to a meeting with Humphrey. The senator told Tom directly, "You have to go home and keep your business alive!" Tom told him that he was committed to him and wanted to do all he could for him to become President of the United States. He said, "Hubert, I just want you to win!" Humphrey looked Tom in the eyes, in what Tom calls "that warm, tender, Norwegian look," and said, "I want you to go back home to Minneapolis and save your business." So Tom returned to Minnesota. Senator Humphrey also asked one of his close friends, Hal Greenwood, to put Tom on the board of his savings and loan company. Tom was the first African-American to hold a position on this board.

In spite of all of Tom's hard work on two campaigns, Humphrey was never elected to the office of President. He did serve as the 38th Vice President under Lyndon B. Johnson.

HUBERT H. HUMPHREY
MINNESOTA

United States Senate
WASHINGTON, D.C. 20510

August 11, 1972

Mr. Tom Tipton
Apartment D-28
2434 Clinton North
Minneapolis, Minnesota 55404

Dear Tom:

Have I already dropped you a note of thanks? If I did,
just accept this as an extra dividend.

Tom, you were a wonderful help to me during the
campaign. I hope that in the days ahead I can be of
some assistance to you. It was a privilege to have
you with me.

As ever,

Your friend,

Hubert H. H.

Hubert H. Humphrey

A treasured letter from a treasured friend

A Growing Business and Growing Family

Tom was able to change his focus from the campaign to return
to Minnesota and to save his business. "I can say now that I really
didn't care about saving the business—that is how much I loved
Hubert Humphrey," he said. With Tom back home attending to
business, Vanguard saw new growth. He was able to secure the
Land O' Lakes account, as well as advertising contracts with

Pillsbury, Hanes Hosiery, Dial Soap, and Armour Foods. Tom's agency was the first black firm to win a multi-million dollar contract from the Navy.

Vanguard contracts with the US Navy

Tom traveled to Haiti in 1973 at the invitation of Reverend Walter Battles of Gospel Church of God in Christ and his wife, Reverend Willa Grant-Battles of Grace Temple Deliverance Center. Walter is predominantly recognized for his mission efforts in the inner city of St. Paul, Africa, and Haiti. He passed away in 1995. Willa's mission work continues in Haiti. Tom toured an orphanage and shelter they supported in Port-au-Prince. He was captivated by the smiles and laughter of the children there but realized that life was not as it should be for those children. One particularly coy young girl caught his attention. As they played back and forth, catching each other's eye, an instant bond was formed. This quiet girl had a bright spirit in her. Tom said, "I'd like to adopt her!" The girl's name was Saintanne.

Saintanne shortly after arriving in the US

Saintanne recalled, "Whenever visitors would come to the orphanage, we were ushered in to sing songs to them. I remember seeing Tom come in. I was very shy. After singing, we went back out to play. I remember being brought back in to meet Tom a second time that same day. In the months after that first meeting, I received many packages of gifts. They told me they were from my father. Early in 1974 they started taking me places—to appointments, to have my picture taken, things like that. One day I had to get all dressed up in my church clothes. They made me say goodbye to all of the other kids there. I didn't know where I was going, but Reverend Walter Battles flew with me from Haiti to Minnesota. When I arrived in Minnesota, my new dad, Tom, was waiting for me at the airport along with his mother, Lucille. He was in a wheelchair because he very recently had surgery. That was March of 1974." Tom's third daughter arrived in Minneapolis at the age of about 11. "She was a wonderful and beautiful girl, but she needed a mother," said Tom. He recruited the support from his friends Jewel and Abel Davidson. Saintanne remembered, "Jewel taught me everything. She was who I recognized and called my mother."

Time in front of the camera — Tom, Beverly and Saintanne

Once again, music was never far from Tom's heart. He was traveling in early 1973 with the rhythm and blues singer Roberta Flack, an old high school friend of Tom's. They were in Atlanta, Georgia, to perform at a concert for the mayor. "I went up to the reception desk at the hotel," said Tom, "and this woman was working behind the counter checking people in. I walked up to Roberta and her husband, and I stood there frozen, whispering to Roberta's husband, 'This woman is gorgeous.'" Tom was able to get her telephone number. That was how Tom met Ernestine Collins, the woman he would marry. A month later, Tom was attending a National Association of Marketing Developers meeting in Nashville, Tennessee, and he called her. After a seven-month courtship, Tom and Ernestine married on May 20, 1974.

As far as weddings go, Tom and Ernestine's wedding was *the* social event in Minneapolis. Three of Tom's groomsmen were stars on the Minnesota Vikings Football Team: Jim Marshall, Carl Eller, and Alan Page. His best men were then-Vice President Walter Mondale—who filled in for Hubert Humphrey, who was quite ill at the time—and Joe Black, who was a pitcher for the Brooklyn Dodgers. Alan Page's son was a ring bearer; everyone chuckled when he walked up the aisle and *back* and had to walk up the aisle a second time. Other notables serving as ushers included George Masko and Earl Brooks of the Pillsbury Corporation, Jim Binger, Wheelock Whitney, Hal Greenwood, Abel Davidson, and Sam Patch. The wedding was held at Westminster Presbyterian Church in downtown Minneapolis, with over 1,500 people in attendance. Gary Hines was the pianist. "One of the most beautiful elements of the service," reflected Tom, "was when my longtime friend and high school classmate from Dunbar, Roberta Flack, sang 'The First Time Ever I Saw Your Face' as Ernestine and I walked into the sanctuary." Tom has stayed in touch with Roberta over the years. Most recently she phoned to sing "Happy Birthday" to him at his seventy-fifth birthday gala.

Roberta Flack and wedding guest

Ernestine was reared in Georgetown, South Carolina. "She came from a wonderful family," said Tom. "They did not have much, but they were wonderful people." Ernestine was shy and lacked self-confidence. "Since I was traveling a lot, I wanted her to have friends—girlfriends in whom she could confide and depend on," said Tom. "After meeting someone like Billy Graham or Robert Schuller, Ernestine would ask, 'How did I do?' She was very unsure of herself." What Ernestine did not tell Tom during their courtship was that her grandmother had told her that black ministers were no good, and that all that they wanted was your money. (As a black gospel singer, Tom would be included in the "no good" category by her grandmother.) Earnestine didn't believe in church, but she would go with Tom.

Just a few short months following Saintanne's arrival, Tom married Ernestine. The marriage was stressed with the conflicts of raising a teenage daughter. In the summer, Saintanne would have her two older sisters' support and company during their visits. When summer ended and Saintanne was left alone, the conflicts with Ernestine began again.

ABC Inc" — Anne (Saintanne), Beverly and Cassandra

Tom admits that he was no angel in his relationship with Ernestine, and eventually they drifted apart. "We were married for almost five years, but as the years passed we became distant and both of us were in great distress. Eventually my daughter Saintanne could not take it anymore and moved out of the house at age seventeen to live with Abel and Jewel Davidson until she graduated from high school." Tom talked about this chapter in his life with great sadness. Ernestine eventually went back to live in South Carolina to take care of her parents, and Tom continued his life of business and singing in Minnesota. "There is little good news in separation and a difficult marriage," he reflected, "but it happened, and it was a part of my life." To make things more difficult for Ernestine, her father suffered a broken back from a tree falling on him. He was in a wheelchair for the rest of his life. This incident further affected Ernestine and her need to help her parents and allowed little time for the good things in life. "I loved her family," said Tom, "and still do to this day." Earnestine's parents have passed away.

Although she returned to live in Minnesota, she and Tom do not communicate with each other. Saintanne Tipton lives in the Twin Cities. She has a college education and she is a preacher and teacher. She presently works with a mission organization in Minneapolis that continues to serve the people of Haiti. Saintanne, Cassandra, and Beverly continue to remain in touch with each other and see each other as often as their busy lives and nationwide travel allow.

In the April 1976 issue of *Black Enterprise,* Tom told about his "mini-vacations," which were all that he could afford to take after his business became successful. He was so busy with Vanguard and working as president of the Association of Market Developers that he could only take one-day vacations at various times throughout the year. He stated his philosophy: "I believe it is the quality of the vacation and not the length that is important." Tom told the interviewer for the article about the advance planning that he would do before his day away. "There are only about six days a year suitable weather-wise for horseback riding in Minneapolis." On his day away, Tom would be up at dawn, down at the stables, and on the trail at sunrise. He would ride until sunset. A full day in a single pursuit would be enough for Tom to get his mind and body back in tune. He owned a horse named Jango and boarded it in the western suburbs.

His life in Minnesota allowed him the opportunity to have his three daughters get to know each other. He enjoyed having his girls visit him in the summers. Like most typical teens, they loved shopping, Tom's big German Shepherd, and going to Valleyfair, which opened in Shakopee in 1976.

Tom and daughters (left to right) Cassandra, Beverly and Saintanne

His music continued with Tom singing at Twins and Viking games, local entertainment venues and churches.

Singing the National Anthem at Metropolitan Stadium

Tom and Minnesota Viking Jim Marshall

Tom had met Chuck Colson in the world of politics in 1968. Following seven months' incarceration for his involvement with the Watergate scandal and a rebirth to Christianity, Colson's career focus was on prisoner rehabilitation and prison reform. He founded Prison Fellowship in 1974. Tom had several opportunities to serve Prison Fellowship with his ministry gift of singing the old hymns throughout the 1970s and 1980s. His music took him inside prison walls with Colson and transformed lives.

From time to time Tom had the opportunity to preach as well as sing to his audiences. He received a Certificate of Ordination from Dominion Church in Arlington, Texas, following the completion of several courses.

Dominion Church

CERTIFICATE OF ORDINATION

The undersigned, hereby certify that
upon the recommendation and request of
Dominion Church,
at Arlington, Texas,
which has had full and sufficient opportunity
for judgment of individual gifts, and after satisfactory
examination in regard to personal Christian
experience, call to the ministry, and views of Bible doctrine,

REV. TOM TIPTON

Was solemnly and publicly set apart and ordained to the work of
THE GOSPEL MINISTRY
By authority and order of Dominion Church at Arlington, Texas on the
5th day of October, 2003

Dr. G.J. Watson, Sr. Pastor, Dominion Church

Dr. Eddie Mitchell, COTR-International

Dominion Church, an Affiliate of Church On The Rock International
Bardin Road, Arlington, TX 76017

CHAPTER FIVE

THE CRYSTAL CATHEDRAL

Kum Bay Ya, My Lord, Kum bay ya;
Kum bay ya, my Lord, kum bay ya.
Kum bay ya, my Lord, kum bay ya;
O Lord, kum bay ya.

"Come by Here"
"Kum Bay Ya"
1930s Spiritual

In the fall of 1977, Tom and Minnesota Vikings players Carl Eller, Alan Page, and Jim Marshall were invited to the Waverly, Minnesota home of Hubert and Muriel Humphrey. The group shared stories of their campaign travels together and talked of life over the past years together in Minnesota. They talked cars. They shared a wonderful meal together. Hubert in his best sense of humor wore a jersey made for him that sported the Vikings colors and logos on the front and those of the Dallas Cowboys on the back—just to antagonize his guests over the upcoming game. The jersey draped his ailing 150 pounds. It wasn't until they were ready to return to Minneapolis that they realized how ill their dear friend was and that this was a goodbye. "We all made the trip home in silence, with tears in our eyes," said Tom.

Hubert Humphrey died of bladder cancer at his home in Waverly on January 13, 1978. His last weeks were spent calling his old political friends and foes. His body lay in state in the rotunda of both the United States Capitol and the Minnesota State Capitol. He is buried in Lakewood Cemetery near Lake Calhoun in Minneapolis. Gerald Ford, Richard Nixon, President Carter, and Vice President Walter Mondale all paid their respects. In the words of his close friend and student in politics Walter Mondale, "He taught us how to live, and finally he taught us how to die."

For Tom Tipton, Hubert Humphrey's death left a void in his heart. Tom remembered flying into Washington and traveling to his hotel. He turned on the TV to hear the news flash that Humphrey had passed away. In a very short time, his phone rang, and it was Hubert's son Skip. Skip said, "Tom, Muriel wants to speak with you." Muriel Humphrey took the phone and said "Tom, you know Hubert loved you." "Well, I loved him too," Tom replied. Skip returned to the phone and asked Tom if he would sing at Hubert's funeral. He told Tom that before Hubert died, he had asked to have Tom sing at his service. As difficult as it was for Tom, he accepted the request and sang "The Battle Hymn of the Republic" at the Minnesota Capitol steps as Hubert's casket arrived to lie in state. He also sang at the family service at House of Hope Presbyterian Church in St. Paul. Bill Perry from Sabathani Baptist Church was his accompanist.

He sang these words from "Goin' Up Yonder" by Walter Hawkins:

> *As God gives me grace, I'll run this race*
> *Until I see my Savior face to face.*
> *I'm goin' up yonder*
> *To be with my Lord.*

Tom also sang and recorded "He'll Understand, and Say Well Done!" by Lucy E. Campbell:

> *O when I come to the end of my journey,*
> *Weary of life, and the battle is won,*
> *Bearing the staff and cross of redemption,*
> *He'll understand and say, "Well done!"*

45RPM Recording of He'll Understand and say Well Done

As fate would have it, what was one of the low points in Tom's life was redeemed through a chance encounter that changed the direction of his future. "It was at Hubert Humphrey's funeral that my friendship with Robert Schuller and my relationship with the Crystal Cathedral began." said Tom. "I had heard about Dr. Schuller's ministry but had not met him or his family." Reverend Schuller had been asked to deliver the eulogy at the service. "I didn't know it at the time, but I was seated next to Arvella Schuller, the reverend's wife, during the funeral service. After the service, she invited me to come to her husband's church the next time I was in California. I said that I would, and within two months I was scheduled to sing in their church and on the television broadcast of *Hour of Power*." This chance meeting at Vice President Humphrey's funeral was the beginning of a thirty-five-year relationship that led to over one hundred appearances on the *Hour of Power* television show. "I felt God laying his hands on me that day of Hubert's funeral," Tom told reporter Dana Parsons for the Orange County *Los Angeles Times* in a December 3, 1995 story. "It felt like Hubert was passing Robert Schuller on to me so that I would go and minister around the world singing the old hymns."

Sometime in the months that followed the funeral, Tom found out that Frank Sinatra had contacted those helping plan the funeral and offered his services to sing at the service. When his offer was refused, Sinatra asked, "Who is singing at the service?" When told "Tom Tipton," Sinatra replied, "Who the hell is that?" and hung up.

In 1979, Tom sold his Vanguard advertising agency and moved to California. He lived on Lewis Street in Garden Grove, where he could remain in close contact with the Crystal Cathedral. Reflecting on his relationship with the famous minister, Tom said, "Life with Bob Schuller has been exciting, spiritually rewarding, and sometimes demanding. Bob and Arvella Schuller, along with their family and the staff and congregation of the Crystal Cathedral, will always hold a place in my heart. They allowed and encouraged me to share my God-given gift of song with their worldwide family."

Tom remembers the first Sunday he sang at the Crystal Cathedral. "I sang 'In The Garden,' and the congregation responded with heartfelt applause. I was so humbled by their response. After the first service, in the elevator while on my way to Robert Schuller's office, I began to cry. I was able to pull myself together for the second service, and following my singing, 2,500 more people stood up and clapped. Again, in the elevator I cried so hard I was heaving. I felt God saying to me, 'Tom, a new journey begins for you. Your life is going to be transformed, and you will sing the great hymns in many incredible countries.'" This was the beginning of a major life change for Tom, as he would sing the old hymns in numerous places around the globe.

Over 100 appearances on the "Hour of Power"

As their relationship grew, Robert Schuller was interested in learning about where Tom Tipton grew up. Schuller was born and raised as a rural Iowa farm boy, about as far away culturally from Washington, DC, as one could get. And so he was curious about his friend's growing years. Tom took Schuller to Washington, where he met Tom's mother. "He wanted to go to my junior high school and my high school," recalled Tom. "My mother had him on her radio show, and I showed him the home where I was born. He seemed to love it." Robert Schuller had been a guest in the White House many times, but this was his first occasion to see the heart of Washington with someone who knew it as home.

Tom's relationship with the Crystal Cathedral and Robert Schuller began to develop more fully and Tom drew upon his marketing skills, and together the men worked on a national advertising campaign for *The Hour of Power* for *Ebony* and *Black Enterprise* magazines.

To this day in Tom's home, there hangs a picture of Tom and Robert H. Schuller sitting together in a library. Above the photo, the title reads: "We Work For *The Hour Of Power* Because *The Hour Of Power* Works For Us.*" As a standalone headline, this ad may appear to some as pretentious, but the advertisement went on to say, "What could a black man who grew up in the Washington ghetto and a white man raised on an Iowa farm have in common? The power of prayer. The power of possibility thinking. The ultimate power of unshakable faith."

We Work For The Hour of Power Because The Hour of Power Works For Us.

What could a black man who grew up in the Washington ghetto and a white man raised on an Iowa farm have in common? Power. The power of prayer. The power of possibility thinking. The ultimate power of unshakable faith.

Before they met, their lives ran along parallel lines. Tom Tipton learned to love quartet gospel singing as a boy in Washington. The young Robert Schuller did the same in Iowa. When Tom began his advertising and marketing service, his largest assets were his faith and courage. Reverend Schuller began his ministry in the

State College where he was a member of the Kappa Alpha Psi fraternity. He served on the board of directors of the National Business League and is past president of the National Association of Market Developers. Tom is also president of his own Minneapolis-based advertising agency. He tithes his services to the Hour of Power. It is his special way of giving.

The Hour of Power is the number one rated* religious television program in the country, reaching over two million people every Sunday. This is, in part, because Tom Tipton believes in Reverend Robert Schuller's mes-

Working together — Tom and Rev. Robert H. Schuller

75

The next paragraph of the advertisement explained: "Before they met, their lives ran along parallel lines. Tom Tipton learned to love quartet gospel singing as boy in Washington. The young Robert Schuller did the same in Iowa. When Tom began his advertising and marketing service, his largest assets were his faith and courage. Schuller began his ministry in the same condition, preaching from the top of the snack stand in a drive-in theater . . . Faith, love, strength . . . all through the power of positive thought. It works for Tom Tipton. Reverend Schuller's *Hour of Power* can work for you."

This positive thinking attitude and the belief in the power of prayer was the bond that Tom and Robert Schuller shared, encouraging many travel and ministry opportunities together. With Dr. Robert H. Schuller's ministry, Tom traveled to Germany, France, Norway, and Holland. With Schuller's son Robert A. Schuller, he traveled to Austria and Switzerland.

Robert A and Donna Schuller with Tom

Tom gathered a lengthy list of music and worship friends from the Crystal Cathedral years. Johnny Carl was the former music director at the Crystal Cathedral and played for Tom in the later years. Johnny had an incredible life of music but also a tragic death, which took Tom deeper and deeper into God's love. Tom considers himself in the company of music greats when he speaks of friends Fred Swan, Don Neuen, Art Scott, Marc Riley, and Keith Reese, as well as the many other staff and special guests he met through *The Hour of Power* over the years. Tom also remarks that Robert H. always had the love of his wife, Arvella, and that she was always at his side as a constant support and encourager.

Travels with Schuller weren't without their challenges. Schuller had a high profile with the media and with the general public, something of a celebrity status. In June of 1997, Tom was invited by Schuller to travel with him to attend the funeral of Betty Shabazz, wife of the late civil rights leader Malcom X. On this particular cross-country flight from California to New York, the men met with an irritable collection of flight attendants in the First Class section of the plane. Several confrontations took place during the flight between Schuller and the attendants over food service, bag stowage, and comfort concerns, and the power struggle resulted in the detention of Tom and Robert by four FBI agents who asked all of the First Class passengers to remain on the plane at the end of the flight. The flight attendants had called for security at New York's JFK airport and falsely reported a physical confrontation between them and Schuller and that charges would ensue. They were held at the airport for four to five hours until one agent was assured that Tom would see to it that Schuller would be at a court appearance the next afternoon. "I knew all of the accusations were false. I was a witness to all that transpired. Someone was looking to make some money off of a high-profile celebrity," said Tom.

Following the funeral for Betty Shabazz, Tom and Schuller went to their hotel for the night. In the morning, in a conference call to his family and staff, Schuller told them all what had happened. In a short period of time, the court appearance was canceled, and a private plane was waiting for them at the airport to return to California. Tom saw the distress of the entire family over this incident, especially Schuller's concern over the media attention and the potential harmful effects on his ministry.

The next morning, Tom was waiting at the Crystal Cathedral when Schuller arrived. Schuller came in the front entrance, and as Tom said, "I saw the most amazing scene that I had ever witnessed in the church. Every person there, all 3,000 of them, had on a button that said, 'Reverend Schuller, your touch blesses me.'" The news media grabbed on to the story like hungry lions going after raw meat. Schuller went on *Larry King Live* to discuss the incident. In the live interview that Tom was watching from home in California, Schuller mentioned that Tom was with him for the trip. Tom immediately packed a bag and hid out from the media in a hotel for three days until the story blew over. In Tom's words, "I was not going to tell the media anything. I knew what really happened, but I was not going to have my words twisted and confused by any reporters. I have a tremendous sense of loyalty to Robert Schuller. He is one of the greatest people I have ever known." The incident was ultimately settled with Schuller pleading not guilty to a misdemeanor charge and paying a small fine.

During Tom's relationship with the Schuller family and the *Hour of Power* ministry, he has witnessed the church at its highest and lowest points. In 1980 the massive, all-glass Crystal Cathedral opened its doors to large crowds of "possibility thinkers" led by Robert H. Schuller. It was a prime time in the ministry, when there was high media success with the publication of Schuller's books and the *Hour of Power* broadcasts. His weekly services were highlighted by special guests, musicians, and dignitaries, all sharing their testimonies of praise. In Tom's opinion, when Schuller had difficulties delivering the right message, he would look to those around him that had a closer view of life's specific trials, and he would draw on their strengths and empowerment to reach his audiences.

Tom tells of returning from a lengthy visit from Australia to sing at the cathedral on a Sunday. This was the weekend of the Rodney King beating and Los Angeles riots. Schuller asked Tom to share his thoughts and views. "He allowed me to take up six minutes of his sermon time, just to share my take on the situation," said Tom.

As Robert H. Schuller looked towards retirement, the congregation looked to his son, Robert A. Schuller, to continue the ministry. Dissension in the family and ministry boards led to the resignation of Robert A. Schuller in 2008, and an apparent downward spiral began. The congregation looked to Robert H. Schuller's daughter for guidance. Sheila Schuller Coleman served as the minister for the congregation until early 2012. Already reeling with the announcement that the Crystal Cathedral had filed for bankruptcy and would be sold, a variety of other leaders have made noble attempts to upright this apparently sinking ship. At the writing of this text, the cathedral has been sold to the Roman Catholic Diocese of Orange and as of June 30, 2013, worship began in the congregation's new church location at 12921 Lewis Street in Garden Grove, California, just down the street from the Crystal Cathedral. The *Hour of Power* television ministry continues its weekly broadcasts and is hosted by Robert "Bobby" V. Schuller, son of Robert A. Schuller and grandson of Robert H. Schuller. Robert H. Schuller and wife Arvella continue to make their home in Orange County. In the liner notes of a 1982 CD cover, Arvella Schuller writes, "We continue to be impressed with the presence of Jesus Christ whenever Tom sings for us. Through his voice, and through his faith—especially his eyes—it is easy to see our Lord's love and faith. We love him, and we know you will be touched by his interpretation of the timeless messages. God has blessed us with Tom Tipton's friendship, his very, very special talent, in the way Tom communicates the gospel of Jesus Christ through his voice . . . and through Tom's expertise in public relations. Bob and I really appreciate all of Tom's tremendous help, and we look forward to many years of serving on Tom's team, in the fantastic work of Jesus Christ, in this country and around the world."

As Tom continues to look at the later years of his music career, he sees 2013 as the final year of performances for *The Hour of Power*, although he hopes to serve this treasured family in their ministry as long as he is needed.

Throughout the 1970s and 1980s, Tom traveled extensively throughout the world with several ministry groups. He spent one month each summer in Australia and New Zealand over seventeen years with Peter and Robina Daniels through Robert H. Schuller's ministry. Peter Daniels is a Christian motivational speaker, author, and international director of Robert Schuller Minsitries, After a troubled childhood and business struggles, Peter attended a Billy Graham Crusade that he claimed turned his life around. He has had a successful career as an entrepreneur. His travels with Tom were in part with Youth for Christ Australia and Youth for Christ International. Tom and Peter have maintained their friendship over the years.

Tom with Peter Daniels

Peter was instrumental in helping Tom produce his CD "Tom Tipton Sings to the World" in 1982. Recorded in Takapuna, New Zealand, the pianist was William Mack and the director was Pater Atkinson. In the CD liner notes, Peter Daniels writes, "When Tom Tipton sings, people stop and listen. Whether on television, in church, or at a concert hall, the unmistakable tones of Tom's rich baritone voice, along with the timeless quality of the hymns he sings, combine to leave a lasting impression on his audiences—wherever and whomever they may be . . . I believe that Tom Tipton's music deserves a place in American culture and history. He is unique in his presentation, dynamic in his personality, and sings directly to the heart of every individual. His music inspires, uplifts, and consoles needy hearts. I wish there were more like him!" The songs on this CD include "This is My Father's World," "Standing in the Need of Prayer," "Deep River," "Danny Boy," "Great is Thy Faithfulness," "Make Us One Lord," "Amazing Grace," "No Deposit No Return," "What A Friend We Have in Jesus," "I'm So Glad," "Ole Man River," "Were You There," and "Kumbaya."

Tom Tipton Sings to the World

Tom met the Reverend Billy Graham through George Wilson, the executive vice president of the Billy Graham Association and headquarters in Minneapolis. Tom was invited to sing at Graham's Washington, DC, Campus Crusade in 1986. It was the first time that a guest soloist was from the city the crusade was held in. Here he again made lasting friendships with Graham's full-time vocalist George Beverly Shea and music director Cliff Barrows.

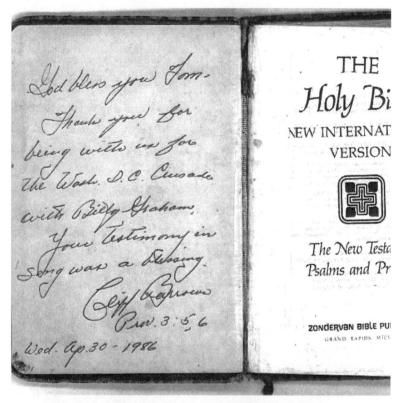

A treasured inscription in Tom's Bible

In 1989 Tom performed with the National Lutheran Choir, under the direction of Larry Fleming. The performance and resulting recording of the CD "Soul" includes folk music, gospel hymns, and spirituals. A CD feature titled "River Suite" includes the songs "There's a Land Beyond the River," "Deep River," and "Down by the Riverside," just to name a few of the seventeen tracks found in this suite.

In the 1990s, the music continued to swell in Tom's life, now stretching over a half century of musical experiences—from the choral classics to the old hymns, from jazz to rhythm and blues, big-band to pop and the contemporary Christian music scene. The release of "Tom Tipton: Hymns from the Heart" was in 1997. Recorded in Portland, Oregon, through the support of Complete Traveler, Inc., and Peggy Palm, the CD includes "Old Time Religion," "Near the Cross," "Shine On Me," "I Need Thee Every Hour," "Faith of Our Fathers," "Every Time I Feel the Spirit," "How Great Thou Art," "I'll Fly Away," "America," "I Heard of a City Called Heaven," "Let My People Go," "Let Us Break Bread Together," and "Doxology." The artistic talents of Billy Wallace on piano, Clay Drayton on bass and keyboards, David Hart on keyboards, Anthony Jones on drums, and vocalists Tami Drayton, Grace Greenidge, and Gerutha Favoral rounded out the musical support. The cover of the CD was painted by Michelin Otis for Tom.

Hymns from the Heart

In 2005, the Crystal Cathedral produced the CD "Shining Out and Shining In." This was by far the most ambitious collection of Tom's music at that time. The selections were all recorded during performances at the Crystal Cathedral over the years and include wonderful arrangements and accompaniment from the Crystal Cathedral Orchestra and Choir. It is hard to pick a favorite from this list: "His Eye is on the Sparrow," "I've Got Peace Like a River," "Every Time I Feel the Spirit," "Make Us One," "What A Friend We Have in Jesus," "This is Church," "Were You There," "Just a Little Talk with Jesus," "He Gives More Grace/Praise Him," "He'll Understand and Say Well Done," "In Shady Green Pastures," "I'm so Glad Jesus Lifted Me," "Knock and the Door Shall be Opened," "Down by the Riverside," "Amazing Grace," "Great is Thy Faithfulness," and "What a Friend We Have in Jesus."

Shining Out and Shining In

CHAPTER SIX

A New Century, A New Home
"My Life Revolves Around
the Old Hymns"

When peace like a river attendeth my way,
When sorrows like sea billows roll,
Whatever my lot, Thou hast taught me to say,
"It is well, it is well with my soul."

"It is Well with My Soul"
Text: Horatio G. Spafford, 1828–1888
Music: Philip P. Bliss, 1838–187

Tom refuses to settle into retirement. He has endured many health issues—multiple back operations, a concussion, spinal meningitis, knee replacements, a detached retina, and a stroke—and at eighty years old, he feels he is living the last chapter of his life. "I truly believe that God has kept me on this earth for a purpose," said Tom, "and He is not finished with me yet!"

In this chapter I hope to share insights into the large world that Tom has experienced, visit with friends that have taken him along on their own personal journeys, and provide some sense of a man that with a handshake brings you into his life, and with a song brings his listeners to life.

Tom returned to Minnesota as a guest in 2003 and 2004 and to stay permanently in Maple Grove in 2005. He went at the coaxing of Bea and Ron Hasselmann. Tom had a long friendship with the couple going back to 1971, when Bea started the Metropolitan Boys Choir. Tom was a guest performer with the choir numerous times and to this day receives a call on his birthday each year with the choir's voices singing "Happy Birthday" from whatever location they are performing at. Ron Hasselmann was the director of the Lord of Life Brass at Lord of Life Lutheran Church of Maple Grove, Minnesota, and invited Tom to sing for the congregation's worship services. He took an instant liking to Maple Grove, the congregation, and the staff and was happy once again to experience firsthand the "Minnesota Nice" he had known during his Humphrey years of the '60s and '70s. Tom's Christmas CD, his tenth recording, was recorded at Easy Street Studio and on location at Lord of Life Lutheran Church in Maple Grove, Minnesota. It was titled "Tom Tipton: Christmas Eve." In addition to accompanists Billy Wallace and David Frank (music director at Lord of Life Lutheran Church), Tom was backed up by the Lord of Life Canticle Choir, directed by Lee Fuchs. Selections included Tom's story of Christmas 1944, "Silent Night," "Joy to the World," "The First Noel," "O Come, O Come Emmanuel," "We Three Kings," "White Christmas," "O Little Town of Bethlehem," "The Christmas Song," "O Come All Ye Faithful," "Ave Maria," "It Came Upon the Midnight Clear" and "O Holy Night."

Tom Tipton: Christmas Eve

"Lord of Life has been a blessing in my life," said Tom, "providing me the support I needed to continue to share the old hymns with those who need to hear them the most."

Tom with Minneapolis Star Trbune columnist Jeff Strickler

Tom does not charge a fee for his performances at senior centers and homes throughout the Upper Midwest. Tom does receive pay in a different form. Writing for the Minneapolis *Star Tribune August 8, 2009* writer Jeff Strickler quotes Tom: "I love to watch the people who are touched by the spirit of songs that give them hope, strength, and faith, and we let them know that someone loves them. I'm more touched than they are. I am blessed to be able to do this."

The gift of music and touch at a senior living center.

As Tom learned over the years, performing and listening to music is an emotional experience. He tells of such an emotional time while singing at a nursing home. "I was performing at an assisted-living center, and this lady started singing along, way off-key. I figured, 'Okay, I'll just keep going.'" She continued to sing with him every song. "Afterwards, one of her attendants told me that she hadn't spoken a single word in several years. These old hymns sparked a fire in her and touched her heart."

Liz Kohman wrote for the *Maple Grove Magazine* in the November/December 2007 issue "Tom Tipton's singing voice is powerful enough to fill up the biggest churches and concert halls around the world, and it has. His personality is engaging enough to attract everyone from politicians to withdrawn elderly living in nursing homes, and it has. His business savvy is keen enough to build a multi-million dollar advertising agency, and it has. But for the past few years, Tipton's talents have aided him on a different sort of mission. He's settled into life in Maple Grove, working with a local church to develop an organization dedicated to bringing music to people in need."

This chapter of Tom's life is focused on those in need of healing. He travels to nursing homes, hospitals, and churches to share his musical gift of singing and to aid in healing those in need of a spiritual message of hope. "This is my calling," said Tom. "This is what God wants me to do, and I will keep doing it as long as I can halfway carry a tune."

Tom is fond of saying that his life "revolves around the old hymns." His two favorite hymns are "His Eye Is on the Sparrow" and "What a Friend We Have in Jesus." These are included in every one of Tom's performances. Because of Tom's love of the old hymns and the heartfelt feeling that he puts into singing each one, he is especially popular with his older audiences. His pastor at Lord of Life Lutheran Church, Peter Geisendorfer-Lindgren, said of Tom, "Sure, they recognize him from TV. But he sings their songs, the old hymns, the ones they sang in church . . . with a heartfelt passion and personal connection to each audience member. This is one of the reasons he is so popular." The personal connection is no more evident than the story of his dear friends Suzanne and James Gaboury. They connected so strongly with Tom and his message that Tom was asked to be godfather to their children Avery and Gunner. For many years they have now called him family, share all of their milestones with him and regularly include him in family activities with their teenage children.

Avery and Gunner Gaboury

On a recent visit to Amarillo, Texas, I had the opportunity to meet with Don Mason, who for years has organized the Realtor's National Prayer Breakfast. He became acquainted with Tom when he called the Crystal Cathedral in California and asked if Tom would come and sing and speak at one of their gatherings. "I was impressed with Tom's sincerity," said Don. "There is nothing phony about him!" Over the years, Tom has been featured at the Realtor's Prayer Breakfast five times and has twice sung at the First Baptist Church of Amarillo, where Don Mason is a member. In talking with Dr. Howard Batson, the senior minister at First Baptist Church, he said about Tom, "He has the amazing ability to cross all barriers. As he walked across the front of the church, he controlled the room. You can see his story in his eyes, and he captures all hearts as he sings and shares that story." In describing Tom's mastery of song, Dr. Batson said, "Tom does not adapt to the song—the song adapts to him."

As Don Mason reflected on Tom's life, he said, "I could see right away that he was not bitter about any past injustices in his life. He could be angry and bitter, but he is not! The moment I met him, I could tell that this is a man filled with the love of God."

Lois Rand, the widow of Sidney Rand (president of St. Olaf College in Northfield, Minnesota, 1963–1980) and ambassador to Norway under President Jimmy Carter, met Tom in the early 1970s. "I first heard him sing at Hubert Humphrey's funeral," she said. Ms. Rand helped to arrange a singing tour for Tom in Norway. "We connected with the ambassador at that time and Tom went, staying as a guest at the embassy." During his time in Oslo, Ambassador Loret Miller Ruppe arranged a dinner date for him. Tom had no idea who his date would be, but he graciously accepted. Tom's date was introduced to him as "Ms. Brown." During dinner at the restaurant, people kept coming up to his dinner partner and greeting her. Suddenly there was a burst of recognition, and Tom blurted out, "You're not Anne Brown of *Porgy and Bess* fame, are you?" Indeed she was. Anne Brown, who was the first to play Bess in the musical, had moved to Norway, marrying a Norwegian many years earlier, to escape the racism she had experienced in the United States. Lois is in contact with Tom on a regular basis and encourages his performing gifts by hosting his concerts in Northfield.

Tom with Lois Rand and her son Mark Ekeren

Dr. Arthur Rouner, the now-retired preaching minister from the Colonial Church of Edina in Minnesota, and his wife, Molly, had Tom as a guest soloist at Colonial Church many times, and they also traveled with Tom on a mission trip. "I traveled to India with Dr. Rouner," said Tom. "In ten days, we preached and sang to over 75,000 Hindus. What a time we had!" Dr. Rouner writes about Tom in these words: "Tom Tipton is my friend. He is not an old schoolmate. We are not pals by profession, nor did we grow up together. We are friends by faith. Tom came to the Twin Cities from Washington and became an advertising executive. I came to the Twin Cities from Boston to teach high-achieving white folks the genius and value of their puritan and pilgrim traditions. In the 1960s many traditions of American life were unraveling. We marched. We schemed. We founded institutions in the city to help people and to build bridges across the lines of difference: halfway houses for prisoners and homes for delinquent girls, nursery schools and street academies. And somewhere in the mix Tom Tipton and I met. Tom was a promoter of people. We met many times to eat together, to talk with one another, and to dream together. Tom called us 'the salt and pepper team.'

Tom and Arthur Rouner

"Wherever Tom would sing, whether at the Metrodome before a Vikings football game, at the Crystal Cathedral on *The Hour of Power,* or in the Colonial Church of Edina, Tom always touched hearts. He would walk the aisles, microphone in hand, and reach out to people by name. They couldn't resist. Always they took the hand he held out to them. He drew people in . . . He drew me in." Dr. Rouner's words of praise for Tom continue: "Tom is an instrument of the Spirit. His songs speak love and peace and convey the spirit of Jesus. While on a singing tour of Australia, Tom called me, and I asked him how he was. He responded, 'It is well with my soul . . . It is well . . . It is well with my soul.' He helped it be well with many souls. He is a winsome 'instrument of His peace' for us all."

"We traveled together to India, and Tom was able to teach me," Dr. Rouner remembered. "At the beginning of this journey, my sermons were something of a disaster. Back in our room in the Kandhari Hotel, Tom said, 'Arthur, what were you thinking, giving that long sermon? You have got to get out from behind that pulpit. You have to show the people your knees. Loosen up and get free!'"

Dr. Rouner stated, "After the crusade meetings, mothers would wait outside for Tom—not me—to bless their children, to lay his hands on them and pray for their healing and for their lives. They saw the Holy Spirit in him. They heard Jesus' call in those wondrous songs he sang so poignantly and so powerfully. There is something in Tom that is forever young. He encourages me and inspires me . . . My salt and pepper friend."

Tom met Dr. Joe Ofstedahl in 2006, when he became one of the doctor's patients. In describing his relationship with Tom, Dr. Ofstedahl said, "We met right at the crux of some major life stresses for me. In fact, at that time my marriage was in the final state of collapse. The timing, given that I was at a very tough point in my own life, was important and very well providential. I did not know who Tom was or what he had done, but I remember he brought a glow of something good into the room with him. Right away you just feel better being with Tom.

"While I have seen Tom a number of times over the years to help take care of his medical needs, it's generally been more the other way in terms of the caretaking," recalled Dr. Joe. "It was Tom taking care of me. I don't think he can help it, actually. The good energy he radiates, that picks up the souls of everyone he meets, mine included, is just natural. It is not surprising that he is so well loved. He is all genuine, no hidden motives or phoniness. Tom shines out and lets the light shine out like very few people do. This is how God made him. He doesn't let himself get in the way of his soul's light, so it really does just shine out, unfiltered like it was created to do.

"Just knowing that he is coming in for a visit makes you feel happy," Dr. Joe remembered. "I can hear him coming down the hall, picking up the staff all the way along. Once, after we had met a few times, I remember coming in the room, and as always, he gave me a big hug and even a bigger smile. This time, I remember he said, 'Hey dude,' and then he said, 'When I say dude, it means love.' I'm not sure he remembers that, but it has stuck with me. Ever since, we have always told each other, 'I love you.' We began to get together just to talk, often over dinner. I've had the opportunity to see Tom sing at events a number of times, from performances at his church to singing the National Anthem at Minnesota Twins games. My favorite was an incredible jazz program he did for friends, backed up by some of the best jazz instrumentalists in the Twin Cities.

"At some point, a few years ago, I remember giving Tom what I think was a Christmas card, and in it mentioning to him, for the first time, how important it was to me that we had met. I remember telling him I met him right when my life Humpty-Dumptied. I am not sure that is a real word, but it gets the point across. That description made him laugh, because if you are Humpty Dumpty, you are broken beyond repair, but then you get a chance to be put back together a better way, leaving the bad pieces where they lay."

Dr. Joe Ofstedahl with Tom

Dr. Ofstedal concluded by stating, "At times I have mentioned to other people about Tom's accomplishments, and after a few minutes I am always astonished at how many there are that know of him—and how the list keeps growing! He is just incredibly good at everything he tries, from business to politics, and his civil rights work as well as his ministry of singing."

Not last and certainly not least on Tom's life list of VIPs is Wheelock Whitney Jr. Wheelock is a well-known Minneapolis businessman and philanthropist who once owned a portion of the Minnesota Twins baseball team and the Minnesota Vikings football team. His background could not be more opposite from Tom's. He attended Phillips Andover and Yale University, where he was a member of Delta Kappa Epsilon fraternity, the same fraternity as President George H. W. Bush. On the surface there are no two men more unalike in social standing and upbringing than Tom and Wheelock. And yet each calls the other "my close friend and brother." A source of inspiration and encouragement

95

to Tom's ministry, Tom said "For more than forty years he has been my big brother." Tom sang at Wheelock's wedding, when he married Kathleen A. Blatz, a former Supreme Court Justice of Minnesota. To this day, each time they meet, they put their heads together to try to out-do each other with lowest bass note they can sing on that particular day. Tom and Wheelock met when Tom was in the advertising business in the late 1960s. Their friendship began when Wheelock asked Tom to work with him on a United Way campaign. Tom accepted, and they have been best of friends ever since. "I became aware that Tom loved to sing," reflected Wheelock. "I flew out to Denver to hear him and encouraged him to give up the advertising business and devote his time to sharing his gift of voice with others. It did not take too much encouragement. Tom did just that!" Today Wheelock Whitney Jr. serves on the Tipton Music Ministries board of directors, along with Tom's pastor, Peter Geisendorfer-Lindgren, David Frauenshuh, and former United States Senator from Minnesota David Durenberger.

Tom with Wheelock Whitney and Kathleen Blatz

Close friends and advisors Peter Geisendorfer-Lindgren, Wheelock Whitney, David Durenberger, David Frauenshuh and Tom

As Tom grew spiritually, his interest in politics changed as well. As the president of the Young Democrats in Washington and his long-time affiliation with Hubert Humphrey, Tom has mostly been associated with the Democratic Party. At this point in his life, however, Tom cares less about political parties and more about the spiritual life of politicians—Democrat or Republican. This is shown by his service to Minnesota governors Wendell Anderson, Rudy Perpich, Al Quie, Arne Carlson, and Tim Pawlenty. Secretary of State Mark Ritchie has become a close friend of Tom's through Tom's performances at several Blue Book presentation ceremonies and the WWII Memorial dedication at the Capitol, as well as Veteran stand-downs, Veteran's Hospital visits, and celebrations and dedications throughout the Twin Cities honoring veterans.

Working with Gov. Wendell Anderson

Tom Tipton Day with Gov. Tim Pawlenty

MN Secretary of State Mark Ritchie & Tom

Tom And George H W Bush

Meeting Hilary Clinton

The Tipton Eight

In this period of his life, Tom is reflective. He said, "When I look back on my childhood, I think about how many times I could have gone wrong. What have I learned over my eighty years, and what can I share with the young people of today? One, to thine own self be true, always! Two, always follow your heart. Three, give everyone the benefit of a doubt. Four, go the extra mile, even though it may hurt. Five, honor your father and mother that their days may be longer. Six, enjoy nature as often as possible. Spend time in the woods, near a lake, and enjoy the animals that are truly God's gifts to us. Seven, exercise for your health, and eight, take time to dream." These "Tipton Eight" could be preached as a sermon every week!

In October of 2010, Tom had a stroke. The events of that day and following weeks have had a great impact on Tom. Having his body fail was frightening. There were so many unknowns. Was this the end?

Friends who had been with Tom in the morning were concerned that he seemed to have trouble walking. Tom's manager, Lori, had already arranged to pick up Tom at noon for a business appointment. "Lori is not only my manager, she is a registered nurse," said Tom. "I was able to walk into the office building slowly, but as I left a few minutes later the ability to move my right leg was gone." Quickly recognizing the signs of a stroke, Lori was on the phone reporting to Dr. Ofstedahl from the car. "She drove me directly to Dr. Joe's office, where they were waiting for me with a wheelchair to be admitted to the hospital," Tom said. After waiting nearly three hours with no exam by a physician or nurse, an ER nurse told Tom that his walking difficulties were "most likely related to your history of back problems." "It took only one look between Lori and me to know we had had enough," said Tom. Tom signed out of the hospital AMA, and Lori drove him back to Maple Grove and the emergency room of the Maple Grove Hospital. He was admitted to the hospital with a diagnosis of a stroke. Tom's recollections of the next few days were foggy at best. He remembered meeting neurologist Dr. Ivan Brodsky, asked to consult Tom's case. After two days of assessments and observation, Tom was transported by van to North Memorial Hospital in Robbinsdale, Minnesota, for rehabilitation. "That night I remember my manager, Lori, at my bedside, but that is all. In the morning when I awakened, the room was filled with physicians and nurses, including Dr. Brodsky. He looked at me very strangely and said, 'Mr. Tipton, we have some problems. First of all, we are going to put a stent in your heart.' I asked why, and he said, 'To keep you alive!'" Tom went through an angiogram and stent placement only after convincing the staff that Lori had to give the okay.

"A voice within me said, 'Be still and know that I am God,'" Tom said. "I remained in the hospital for three weeks for physical and occupational therapy. They worked me out every day." He was very grateful for visits from pastors Peter and Karen, as well as "my dear friends Wheelock Whitney and David Frauenshuh, who seemingly kept a vigil at my bed until I was up and moving again. I did not know anything except that I was glad to be alive." By the time Tom was discharged, he was walking several times around the therapy department with the use of a cane and had regained sensations and use of his right hand and leg except for some mild weakness. He returned to his home, and after a few more weeks of therapy has been able to live independently since then.

Months before his stroke, Tom had made a commitment to travel to Asheville, North Carolina, to sing at The Cove, the Billy Graham Ministry training center, which was arranged by Dell Moore, Cliff Barrows' private secretary. He was to be a part of a senior ministry conference. Tom did not want to concern his friends at the Billy Graham event, but a newspaper story brought them the news anyway. Tom spoke with his friend Cliff Barrows and assured him that he would do everything humanly possible to make the event—and he did.

Tom with Cliff and Ann Barrows

In April of 2011, Tom had regained his strength and felt able to travel. He made the trip to Asheville, where he sang before three hundred people for four days straight. On more than one occasion, Tom sang a duet with a then-101-year-old George Beverly Shea. On the last evening of the conference, the attendees were surprised by a special guest. Cliff Barrows and George Beverly Shea were conversing on stage about some of their life experiences when the side door opened. Being pushed through the doorway in a wheelchair by his daughter was Billy Graham. Looking frail but filled with a strong spiritual presence, Graham waved to a standing ovation from the audience. With a big smile on his face, he sang an old hymn or two along with the crowd. And then Cliff Barrows invited Tom to stand and sing to the great evangelist, suggesting that Tom sing "Precious Lord."

***Cliff Barrows and George Beverly Shea at the
BGEA Senior Conference***

Forgetting his cane and feeling strong enough to move without it, Tom stood and grabbed a microphone, while the pianist began the introduction to "Precious Lord." Looking Dr. Graham in the eyes, Tom began, "Precious Lord, take my hand. Lead me on, help me stand. I am tired, I am weak, I am worn." At the end of the first verse, Cliff Barrows encouraged Tom to sing the second verse as well. As Tom began, Billy Graham reached for Tom's hand. "Hear my cry, hear my call. Hold my hand lest I fall. Take my hand, precious Lord, lead me home." By the time Tom's solo to Graham was completed, there was not a dry eye in the assembly hall, including those of Billy Graham and Tom Tipton.

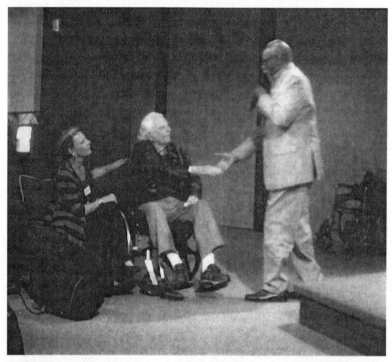

Take My Hand moment with Tom and Rev. Billy Graham

In this, the autumn of Tom's life, he was especially grateful for an invitation from the community of Wayzata, Minnesota, to speak at their annual Community Prayer Breakfast, held at the Wayzata Country Club in October 2011. "About three hundred people gathered for breakfast and to hear me share my spiritual journey," said Tom. It was Paul Webster, Toby Piper, Kathy Tunheim, and Paul and Jerry Jones, longtime Wayzata residents, who asked Tom to share his story. "The morning was filled with old friends, new friends, people who had heard Tom Tipton the hymn singer and who knew him as a business persons or politician," said Tom. "I saw faces of people I hadn't seen in years, but they came to celebrate life and to celebrate love."

One of those attending the breakfast was former Congressman Jim Ramstad. Congressman Ramstad said of Tom, "Tom has touched literally hundreds of thousands of people across the world as 'America's favorite hymn singer.' Tom has been a brother and friend to me since we first met in the early 1980s at the Minnesota Prayer Breakfast. I was absolutely mesmerized by this gifted gospel singer and his rendition of 'Amazing Grace.' I was even more profoundly impacted by his deep and abiding faith.

"Tom Tipton has truly lived the admonition that, 'Here on earth, God's work must be our own.' From prayer breakfasts and Billy Graham Crusades to senior centers, youth audiences, and Robert Schuller's *Hour of Power,* Tom has been an inspiration to people around the world from all walks of life. People like former Vice President of the United States Hubert H. Humphrey and retired maintenance chief Abel Davidson. People like Minnesota Twins legend Kirby Puckett and Imogene Maborne, a retired public relations consultant. No person who attended the funerals of Vice President Humphrey or Kirby Puckett could ever forget the booming baritone of Tom Tipton singing our favorite hymns, without a dry eye at either service.

"As the co-chair with my beloved wife, Kathryn Ramstad, of the fiftieth anniversary of the Minnesota Prayer Breakfast in 2010, Tom Tipton's memorable singing was the highlight to an overflow crowd, just as it was to our family and friends at my dad's funeral the year before.

"As a member of the United States Congress for eighteen years, I could always count on Tom's faithful counsel on issues affecting 'the least amongst us.' His loyal friendship and prayerful advice have been major blessings in my life, just as he has been a shining example of a servant leader to all of us who know and love him."

At a gathering with the late Paul Wellstone and Jim Ramstad

Roger Williams, world-renowned pianist to most of us, was a best friend to Tom Tipton. They met when Tom was a guest on *The Hour of Power*, where they both continued to make many appearances over the years. For many years of their friendship, Roger fondly called Tom "son," and Tom would always reply with the same affection to "dad," even though Roger was less than ten years Tom's senior. They spoke to each other weekly. When Tom had his stroke, Roger called to check on him regularly. The same was true of Tom checking in on Roger as he battled with pancreatic cancer the last months of his life. Tom treasures the photo on his wall of him and Roger standing at the piano—the photo being a birthday gift sent to him by Jacque Heebner, Roger's lifelong friend and manager. Roger died in October of 2011. Tom's friend and manager Lori Schwartz remembered a weekend that Tom spent visiting Roger in California to be grand marshals in a community parade. Tom called Lori's home in Minnesota and said, "Hold the phone, someone wants to talk to you." In a few seconds she heard the laughter of the men as Roger took the phone and jokingly said, "Hi Lori, this is Roger Miller!" She could picture the two sitting across the table from each other just talking about everyday life and business. "There is a price for notoriety, and I think Tom and Roger both understood that and were able to escape that world with each other and enjoy a simpler life even if for a few days at a time," said Lori. Tom was able to travel to California to eulogize his friend and share his songs at the private memorial service in Thousand Oaks, California, the public remembrance at the Nixon Library in Yorba Linda, and the interment service at the Crystal Cathedral Memorial Gardens in Garden Grove, California.

Roger Williams and Tom Tipton

Brigadier General Dennis Schulstad introduced Tom to David Frauenshuh in 2007. Tom regularly performed at veterans' events throughout Minnesota at the invitation of Dennis. Both men have served on Tom's board of directors and have been faithful ministry supporters and encouragers.

Tom was honored to sing at the National Baseball Hall of Fame Museum on July 27, 2006. Tom also sang the National Anthem at the Ozzie Smith "Play Ball" event. Tom had the opportunity to meet the Negro League's great John "Buck" O'Neil.

Hallof Fame photo (left to right): Ozzie Smith, Steve Solmonson, Ryne Sandberg, Tom Tipton, George Brett, Rev. Peter Geisendorfer-Lindgren and John "Buck" O'Neil

The request for Tom to sing in Cooperstown was generated from contacts at the Hall of Fame through local friend Steve Solmonson. Solmonson and Pastor Peter Geisendorfer-Lindgren had attended the funeral service for the Minnesota Twins legend Kirby Puckett, where Tom had been invited to sing. "I didn't know Kirby personally," said Tom, "but had met him through

Rod Carew and Dave Winfield. I was honored to serve the Twins organization to sing at Puckett's service."

The "Sounds of Freedom and Faith" CD produced by the Crystal Cathedral was released in 2007. This glorious music celebrated the positive freedom of the human spirit. In addition to Tom's rendition of "God Bless America," other artists included Dorothy Benham (Miss Minnesota 1976 and Miss America 1977), Daniel Rodriguez, Lee Greenwood, and Wintley Phipps.

Tom's good friend Denny McGrath is an incredible human being, a loving husband and a brilliant speaker. "He knows how to make things happen," said Tom, "and has been there for me since day one." Denny is a communications consultant for the Archdiocese of Saint Paul and Minneapolis Roman Catholic Church of Minnesota. Dennis connects with Tom as his own Irish brother, and over the years they have made rituals out of St. Patrick's Day celebrations. Denny has been a constant encourager and career support for Tom, often organizing events and appearances for Tom as well as consulting on promotional materials. On one such occasion, *The Irish Gazette* newspaper of St. Paul said in its June 2009 edition article by Jenny Simonsen, "Tom Tipton's voice begins somewhere near his toes and bellows up to turn heads even when he is not singing a beloved gospel hymn. The baritone deepness of his voice is indeed enthralling, but not as much as his charismatic attitude noting kinship of all people regardless of ethnic or racial background." Tom sang "A Cottage in Old Donagle" for those gathered at the local Irish pub. Peter Link, producer of Tom's CD "The best of Tom Tipton," recalled, "An African-American man singing an Irish air? Made a believer out of me. Tom puts you in the green hills of Ireland on a moonlit night in the spring. He puts you there, goosebumps and all." Denny McGrath and Debbie Estes were the key organizers of Tom's 75th Birthday Gala, bringing together 300 of Tom's most treasured friends and family.

Debbie and Ralph Estes with Tom

Dennis McGrath and Tom

All of this leads us to Tom's most recent CD, produced by Peter Link and Watchfire Music in 2008. "The Best of Tom Tipton" not only includes old favorites but some new arrangements as well. Tom recorded this CD at the Watchfire studios in New York City in 2008. A full lineup of nineteen songs includes "What a Wonderful World,"

"Let My People Go," "Every Time I Feel the Spirit," "Goin' Home," "Lord Listen to the Children/What a Friend," "Be Still My Soul," "Amazing Grace/I'll Fly Away," "I Believe," "Near the Cross," O Come, O Come Emmanuel," "Precious Lord," "This is My Father's World," "The Old Rugged Cross," "Kumbaya," "Old Time Religion," "How Great Thou Art," "O Come All Ye Faithful," "Sometimes I Feel Like a Motherless Child," and "A Cottage in Old Donagle."

The Best of

Tom Tipton

Watchfire ♪ Music

Watchfire's cd The Best of Tom Tipton

Lori Schwartz, has had the opportunity to travel over the past five years with Tom to prayer breakfasts, nursing homes, monument dedications, funeral services, appointments, elementary classrooms, worship services, building dedications, concerts, and sporting events. "Tom has shown me so many glimpses of American and Minnesota history and introduced me to hundreds of people who have played very significant roles in that history making," said Lori. "I am sure that many readers may think, 'Was he really friends with all of these people?' I can confirm that with a resounding yes! Just when you think perhaps a casual acquaintance was all he made, those individuals will seek out Tom to shake his hand and greet him with a hug, truly like a long-lost friend. I know that he has genuinely touched the hearts of all the people he has talked about in these memoirs. Tom has also been a teacher of real-life music history. Many miles together in the car have found us challenging each other to music trivia, name that tune, and who-sung-its. Sometimes he simply tunes in to the tight harmonies of groups from then and now as a way to decompress from the stress of performing or the battle of chronic pain and an aging body that sometimes rebels from a hard life of sports and travel. Tom has also inspired my faith, and I have been fortunate to see the light he brings to the faces of those who need to hear that God loves them and He is not finished with them yet. Tom tells them, 'You need to talk to your children, grandchildren, and great-grandchildren. You are needed here on this earth every day to love each other.' Let me also tell you that the light Tom exudes reflects right back on his own face. He is fed by his service to others. It is hard work. It drains his energy. But there is nothing else in this world that he would rather do. He often quotes his favorite scripture from the Old Testament book of Micah, 6:8, 'He has told you, O mortal, what is good; and what does the Lord require of you but to do justice, and to love kindness, and to walk humbly with your God.'"

Tom with Lord of Life office friends Jane Bergstrom and Lori Schwartz

Pastor Peter Geisendorfer-Lindgren of Lord of Life Church writes, "I first met Tom Tipton when 'the Old Hymn Singer' came to our church as a special guest one Sunday morning to sing for all three services. Ever the professional, he asked what I wanted him to do and where he would be singing in the services. I explained that we had two slots for special music and that I had a lot of other things to fit in, including my sermon, so I asked if he would do two songs and keep the talking to a minimum, I would appreciate it. An hour later he had performed three songs, told four stories and shook hands with half the congregation. As we strode down the center aisle during the recessional, he asked if it was okay. I said, 'Don't change a thing.' I could cut my sermon, because the church hears me talk every week, but hearing Tom Tipton sing is a special gift from God.

"That was almost ten years ago now, and it would not be an exaggeration to say that my life was changed that day. Since then, we have traveled across the country together, visited scores of nursing homes, gone to numerous sporting events where Tom sang the National Anthem, and imbedded ourselves in each other's families.

"Tom has an amazing story. He never became bitter or angry because of the prejudice he endured. Like Daniel in the Old Testament, Tom overcame many obstacles to accomplish great things: to be an organizer for the March on Washington, to own and operate the Vanguard advertising agency, to sing for presidents, to be the principal soloist for *The Hour of Power* television show, and to appear at Billy Graham Crusades.

"In the last decade, while most men his age are putting their feet up or chasing around a little white ball, Tom began a new ministry. He and I were often a backward 'Driving Miss Daisy,' with me being more than happy to play the role of Morgan Freeman. I was the driver and sound tech, and Tom was an angel sent from God.

"Amazing things would happen in those visits. Tom has the unique ability to identify the person who is hurting in the crowd and reach out and touch them with his hand and sing to them with his voice. Tom would sing his favorite old hymns, and you can see eyes come alive with the recognition of the song and the hope implicit therein. I saw God at work and was more than a little amused by the number of ninety-year-old women who proposed marriage.

"I wish I had known Tom when we both were younger, but I am most grateful to God for these past ten years. Tom has brought a richness to my life that I never would have known. He has been a blessing to my family and our church. When he sings 'Amazing Grace' before Thanksgiving dinner or 'His Eye is On the Sparrow' at Sunday morning church, I almost always reflect on how thankful I am to know Tom. Whatever the future holds for him, my advice would be, 'Don't change a thing. Let your smile warm the faces of all you meet, let your voice proclaim the wonders of God, let your heart declare your love for humankind, and let your arms continue to embrace me as your brother and your friend.'"

Peter Geisendorfer-Lindgren, Tom and Wheelock Whitney

At age 80, Tom continues to travel across the US to visit family and friends, he continues to make new friends daily, he continues to share his ministry of music and he continues to praise and walk humbly with his God.

Tom with college friend Charles MacMillan

Daughter Beverly with her husband Drew Hammond

Tom with his grandsons

Tom's daughter Saintanne

Tom with daughter Cassandra and Kelvin Pye,
grandsons and daughter Beverly

Saintanne and Beverly

Pianist Billy Wallace

Tom with his Aunt Hilda and brothers Arthur and Reggie

Lois Rand with daughter-in-law Joan Ekeren

Tom with David Frauenshuh and Warren and Mary Lynn Staley

Epilogue

"Shining In"

Hear my cry, hear my call,
Hold my hand lest I fall;
Take my hand, precious Lord,
Lead me home.

"Precious Lord Take My Hand"
Thomas A. Dorsey, 1938

"I guess it is easy for those who have never felt the stinging darts of segregation to say wait. But when you have seen vicious mobs lynch your mothers and fathers at will and drown your sisters and brothers at whim, when you have seen hate-filled policemen curse, kick, brutalize, and even kill your black brothers and sisters with impunity . . ."

I was reading from the book *Letter from Birmingham Jail* by Martin Luther King Jr. Tom Tipton sat and listened to the words I was reading, words that had touched me deeply many years ago: "When you see the vast majority of your twenty-million Negro brothers smothering in an air-tight cage of poverty in the midst of an affluent society . . . when you are humiliated day in and day out by nagging signs reading 'white' men and 'colored'; when your first name becomes 'nigger' and your middle name becomes 'boy' (however old you are) and your last name becomes 'John,' and when your wife and mother are never given the respected title 'Mrs.'; when you are harried by day and haunted by night by the fact that you are a Negro, living constantly at tip-toe stance, never quite knowing what to expect next, and plagued with inner fears and outer resentments; when you are forever fighting a degenerating sense of 'nobodiness'; then you will understand why we find it difficult to wait."

As I read these words, Tom's mind went back through his own personal history, the experiences he had been through. He remembered that first Easter Egg Hunt and the rejection which followed. He recalled the process he had gone through in order to survive the kind of prejudice that Martin Luther King Jr. had described. "At first I was hurt," said Tom. "And then I wanted to fight it. When I realized that I couldn't beat it, I had to rise above it." To rise above the prejudice and discrimination in our society was a test of Tom's will, but he has passed the test. Tom also recalled that time in 1968, following the assassination of Dr. King, when the streets of Washington were burning. Tom, as the president of the Young Democrats of Washington, was working with community leaders to help stop the burning. "I stood on the corner of 14th and U street with Marion Barry, Congressman Walt Fauntroy, and others, trying to stop the destruction of our neighborhood."

In Plato's *Republic* there is a conversation that takes place between Socrates and Cephalus. Socrates is reported as saying, "There is nothing which for my part I like better, Cephalus, than conversing with aged men, for I regard them as travelers who have gone on a journey which I too may have to go, and of whom I ought to inquire whether the way is smooth and easy, or rugged and difficult . . . Is life harder towards the end?" The old man replied to the inquiry of Socrates by saying, "Old age has a great sense of calm and freedom."

"Shining in"—in one sense, this is descriptive of Tom moving from shining shoes outside the White House to singing inside— shining in—the White House. In a far deeper sense, however, it is descriptive of the developmental change that has taken place within Tom, a change that has been transformational. It has been his journey. At eighty years of age, Tom is still singing and sharing his message of hope and encouragement. In contrast to his earlier years, however, when he was hurrying here and there, trying to keep a business, a family and his singing career all going at once, he does so now, in the words of the old man's response to the question of Socrates, "with a sense of calm and freedom, joy and inner peace." Tom has some health difficulties, and he does not move as fast or as easily as he once did. These problems, however, do not damage his heart and spirit, nor do they harm his beautiful voice.

True to his word, many years later, complete with memories of his shoe-shining days outside its gates, Tom was invited *inside* the White House and sang for President Jimmy Carter (Tom had also sung for him in Wayzata, Minnesota). He came back to the White House a second time for a Christmas performance for President Bill Clinton. And he was called *Mr. Tipton!*

"*Shining In*" in the White House in 1995

It was Samuel Johnson who wrote, "Vernal flowers, however beautiful and gay, are only intended by nature as preparatives to autumn fruits." Tom is in the autumn years of his life, and he is gathering the fruits of his lifetime of experience. "I am still here," he said. "I must still have a purpose." For Tom, that purpose is to continue to sow the seeds of hope and encouragement wherever he goes and to all who will listen. He is, indeed, a living national treasure.

About the Author

James (Jim) R. Newby is the senior minister of the Church of the Savior, a United Church of Christ and Presbyterian USA union congregation in Oklahoma City. He is also the director of the Trueblood Yokefellow Academy for Applied Christianity (an interdenominational organization committed to individual and church renewal). Jim was born in Minneapolis, Minnesota, and grew up in Muncie, Indiana. He is the son of a Quaker minister. Prior to coming to Oklahoma in 2008, Jim served as the minister for faith and learning at the Wayzata Community Church (United Church of Christ) from 2003 to 2008 in the Twin Cities, and as the minister of spiritual growth at Plymouth Congregational United Church of Christ in Des Moines, Iowa, from 1997 to 2003.

Jim is a member of the Religious Society of Friends (Quaker) and has served as a pastor among Friends in Nebraska, Ohio, and North Carolina. He has been the editor of *Quaker Life Magazine,* and served on the faculty of the Earlham School of Religion in Richmond, Indiana, for ten years. Jim holds degrees from Princeton Theological Seminary (Doctor of Ministry), William Penn College (Doctor of Divinity), Earlham School of Religion (Master of Divinity), and Friends University (Bachelor of Arts). He is the author of numerous books and articles on religious and spiritual subjects, primarily dealing with renewal. His last book, *Sacred Chaos: One Man's Spiritual Journey Through Pain and Loss,* was released by Continuum Group Publishers of New York.

Jim has assumed leadership in the international Yokefellow Movement since the death of his mentor, D. Elton Trueblood, to whom he dedicated his book *Gathering the Seekers* and whose biography he wrote in 1990. Jim is the president of the D. Elton Trueblood Yokefellow Academy Endowment, Inc.

Jim is married to Elizabeth Salinas Newby, author of *A Migrant With Hope* and a specialist in matters concerning immigration. She is the former administrator of the Division of Latino Affairs for the State of Iowa, serving under former Governor Vilsack, who is now the Secretary of Agriculture in the Obama administration. They have one daughter, Alicia Marie Clark, who lives with her husband, David, near Hudson, Wisconsin.

For relaxation, Jim likes to play golf, sail, and walk, as well as spend time at Newbeginnings, his home with Elizabeth on the coast of North Carolina.

About the Book

It is a privilege to share through the ministry of writing this remarkable life with others. The life of Tom Tipton begins as a child in segregated Washington, DC; travels through the powerful music world of jazz, gospel music, and the old hymns; reaches into politics and the struggles and hopes of desegregation; explores worldwide evangelism; and is still being lived out in 2013 in the Twin Cities of Minnesota. It would be a mistake to suppose that Tom Tipton's biography is just one more in the array of books that represent the cult of personal exposure. His is different in kind. His message is one of encouragement to the thousands of people who are now discouraged. His story belongs in one sense to the literature of witness, but in a far deeper sense, it belongs to the literature of hope. It is my hope that those who read these words will have their own lives enriched, in the same way that Tom Tipton has enriched so many lives through his ministry of music. He is an amazing man who has the gift of bringing out the best in others. Prepare for a spiritual experience.

CPSIA information can be obtained at www.ICGtesting.com
Printed in the USA
BVOW07s1705211013

334158BV00003B/5/P